MICHAEL STITSWORTH
4-H Department
AGAD   Room 228
Purdue University
West Lafayette, IN 47907
USA

Bring
Home
the World

Bring
Home
the World

A MANAGEMENT GUIDE FOR
COMMUNITY LEADERS OF
INTERNATIONAL EXCHANGE PROGRAMS

Stephen H. Rhinesmith

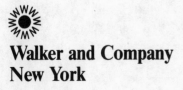

Walker and Company
New York

Copyright © 1985 by the United States Information Agency

This edition first published in the United States of America in 1985
by the Walker Publishing Company, Inc.

Library of Congress Cataloging in Publication Data

Rhinesmith, Stephen H.
  Bring home the world.

  Includes bibliographies.
  1. Exchange of persons programs, American—Management.
I. Title.
E744.5.R47   1985   303.4'8273'0068   85-13730
ISBN 0-8027-7289-7 (pbk.)

Book Design by Teresa M. Carboni

Printed in the United States of America

10 9 8 7 6 5 4 3 2 1

To

Rachel Andresen
Dwight Eisenhower
William Fulbright
Stephen Galatti
and
Donald Watt

*whose collective vision of the possibilities of international
exchanges have enabled hundreds of thousands of us to*

Bring Home the World

Preface

Dr. Charles F. MacCormack, President
The Experiment in International Living

The five people to whom this book is dedicated—Donald Watt, William Fulbright, Stephen Galatti, Rachel Andreson and Dwight Eisenhower—each directed vision, leadership, commitment, and practicality to the strengthening of international exchanges for peace. Donald Watt founded The Experiment in International Living in 1932, driven by his concern that the destruction he had witnessed during the First World War was about to be released on yet another generation. After the Second World War, Galatti became the driving force behind American Field Service; Andreson behind Youth For Understanding; Fulbright behind the Fulbright Program; and Eisenhower behind People-to-People. Each one of these individuals recognized in a profound and personal way that the devastation of modern war called for nations and peoples to find new approaches in dealing with one another.

Each of these five individuals lived through the great world wars of this century; each of them recognized that by far the best medicine for modern war is preventive rather than curative. They were all hard-headed builders of institutions who came to the idea of in-depth exchanges between citizens of different nations as one of the few practical ways of reducing the lack of communication and understanding that is so often the cause of international conflict.

Their specific backgrounds varied immensely, ranging from commanding general of the greatest military force the world has ever known to small town social worker with a new idea. In spite of these vastly different experiences, however, the "founding five" of international citizen exchange had a great deal in common in the way they worked to build the programs on which the whole field is now based. They had a driving vision of why educational exchange was vital to the well-being—perhaps the very survival—of humanity, as well as a great capacity to communicate that sense of significance and that vision to others. They were not concerned with narrow organizational issues, but rather with creating a world of exchanges among peoples that would literally bring about "peace through understanding." They were able to take this personal vision and pass it on to tens of thousands of others in a way that was deeply motivating. And, along with this sweeping sense of purpose, they were able to guide the nuts and bolts of board development, fund-raising, program design, publicity, and financial management in such a way as to create institutions that to this day remain leaders in the field of international educational exchange.

It seems to me particularly fitting to begin a book on the leadership and management of international exchange programs by reflecting on the qualities of some of the "heroes" who created the movement—a movement that today involves millions of people in in-depth intercultural communication each year. The world has changed a great deal in the fifty years since community-based international exchange first began, with a bare handful of participants, and our knowledge of leadership, management and volunteer motivation has changed also. Nevertheless, it is worth noting that the basics—a deep sense of mission, the ability to communicate that sense of mission to others, a concern for quality and integrity, and a willingness and ability to understand the details of planning, finances, fund-raising, program content and publicity—have been concerns of those who led in the field of educational exchange from its founding.

The core idea of educational exchange—that common knowledge, insight, skills, and fellowship among peoples of different languages and cultures can reduce some of the causes of international conflict—is even more important in our own era of nuclear confrontation and Third World political instability than it was when Donald Watt founded The Experiment in International Living or Dwight Eisenhower established People-to-People. Additionally, as the field has expanded to involve millions of people and billions of dollars each year, the ultimate importance of the cause makes it imperative that those scarce resources are effectively spent. It is fortunate that international exchange was established by a group of brilliant natural leaders, but unless their commitment, dedication and practicality can be replicated by thousands of others throughout this nation and around the world, H. G. Wells's "race between education and catastrophe" might well be lost.

Bring Home the World, by Dr. Stephen Rhinesmith, Past President of the American Field Service and an indispensable leader in the "successor generation" of citizen exchange, is an invaluable resource in the ongoing effort to enable international educational exchange to achieve its full potential in a volatile and interdependent world. It is not a simple book, any more than the effort to provide genuinely effective international leadership at the local level is a simple effort. What *Bring Home the World* does, in essence, is synthesize the best of two decades of research and publication on organizational dynamics, corporate culture, nonprofit management techniques, and cross-cultural behavior and apply them to the field of international exchange.

The book is not a manual that describes how to carry out the mechanics of international exchange, but rather a summary of the basic philosophy, principles, concepts and practices involved in leading people and organizing collective effort toward a larger vision. It begins with the fundamentals of human communication, examining the humanistic insights of thinkers such as Carl Rogers for their relevance to motivating human beings and communicating across cultures. For many international volunteers, the philosophical and conceptual sweep of *Bring Home the World* will be somewhat breathtaking. There is, after all, a rather wide intellectual leap to be made from humanistic psychology and the social transformations of post-industrial society to homesick Latin American teenagers, overcrowded high school classrooms, and turning out volunteers for local fund-raisers.

Nevertheless, it is one of the central, and in my opinion correct, assumptions of the book that it is ultimately vision, mission and purpose that is the *sine qua non* of successful leadership and management of community-based educational exchange efforts. Today's world faces unparalleled challenges and opportunities in the realms of arms control, the environment, population, social justice and economic development. Avoiding problems and seizing opportunities in each of these areas is going to require a degree of international understanding and cooperation that we are certainly not seeing currently. The thousands of community volunteers working for international exchange around the world will ultimately have failed as leaders if millions of individuals are only moved from one country to another, without elevating the sights of those involved to the need for more informed and more disciplined citizen action on world issues.

In this regard, the chapter on "Exchange Visitors as Global Educators" is especially important. Each year tens of thousands of non-American exchange students enter U.S. high schools, and additional tens of thousands of American students study and learn abroad. These large-scale exchanges have been going on for years, yet the international interest and competence of most American schools and communities shows little indication of systematic improvement. It is essential that those working at the community level for international awareness through exchange join the growing effort to improve America's global competence, and *Bring Home the World* offers a number of practical suggestions on how to do this.

The past two or three years has seen the publication of a growing body of literature on intercultural communication in general and citizen exchange in particular. We are witnessing the development of a more informed discipline of international educational exchange, drawing on the decades of practical experience of millions of international volunteers, host families, and adult and youth exchange participants. *Bring Home the World* can be seen as the centerpiece of this growing discipline, in the sense that it provides an overall synthesis of what we have learned about leadership, management, intercultural communication and international exchange.

The bibliographies at the end of each chapter are particularly valuable as a guide on where to go next for the reader who needs more information of a specialized sort. The book can profitably be read by a number of audiences in the citizen exchange field: board members, professional staff, volunteer leaders, concerned educators, and host families. Different groups will want to focus on one or more of the book's varied themes—management philosophy and theory, trends in international education and exchange, techniques of community institution-building—that are most appropriate to their particular needs.

It is the particular role of *Bring Home the World* to present a synthesis of both the why and the how of leadership for international understanding. Rachel Andreson, Dwight Eisenhower, William Fulbright, Stephen Galatti and Donald Watt provided a great many people with living examples of how this can be done. The challenges and opportunities of today's world furnish thoughtful people everywhere with many of the same concerns and aspirations these leaders were responding to. *Bring Home the World* offers a framework for making a practical and personal commitment to leadership for a small planet.

Contents

**PART II:
MANAGING YOUR RESOURCES:
PEOPLE, PROGRAMS AND FINANCES**

**PART III:
MANAGING THE CROSS–CULTURAL EXPERIENCE:
CULTURE SHOCK, COUNSELING,
AND GLOBAL EDUCATION**

**PART IV:
MANAGING RENEWAL: OF YOURSELF,
YOUR ORGANIZATION, AND OTHERS**

List of Figures

Introduction

This is a management guide for community leaders of international exchange programs. Let's take a moment to outline exactly what that means.

First of all, what follows is a "management guide." Basic "management" activities such as planning, organizing, staffing, leading, and controlling are described in terms of their applicability to an organization of local community volunteers. This book is a "guide," because I have tried to include examples, strategies, exercises, and instruments that you can use in carrying out your responsibilities in your local organization.

Second, this is a management guide for community leaders. The translation of "community leaders" is "local volunteers." The international exchange movement in the United States has grown through the years since the Second World War because thousands of community volunteers have given millions of hours of time to local schools, service clubs, and visitors' programs to help people from abroad discover life in American villages, towns, and cities. Likewise, they have worked to raise funds and select representatives to go abroad, learn about people in other countries, and report back to local communities their impressions of life in different parts of the world.

Volunteers involved in international exchange have found that their organizations have grown over the last forty years, and that the processes of raising money and obtaining publicity have become more difficult. In addition, competition for the scarcest resource of all—new volunteers—has increased to the point where volunteer leaders need some specialized information and techniques about how to manage their local groups. This guide is intended to provide basic information about how to recruit, organize, and motivate volunteers to work for international exchanges.

Finally, the important and distinguishing aspect of this book is that it is written exclusively as a management guide for community leaders of "international exchange programs." It is this last characteristic which I hope will make this book a unique contribution to the general management literature available today.

In the last fifteen years a number of fine books on volunteer management have been published. Names like Harriet Naylor, Joan Flanagan, and others are well known. In addition, many volunteer organizations have started management training programs to enhance their volunteers' ability to manage people, programs, and finances under increasing competition and complexity.

What has not been done before, with the exception of the first edition of this book, is the publication of a management guide that addresses some of the more specific needs of volunteers in international exchange. This book attempts to fill this need with chapters on the purposes of international exchange and more specialized chapters on culture shock and cultural adjustment, cross-cultural counseling, and the role of international exchange and global education in our school systems today.

For this reason, I hope that you, as a local volunteer in the international exchange field, will find this guide particularly useful. While I have addressed this to the "presidents" of local volunteer groups, almost any volunteer should find portions that are helpful. In addition, professional staff who work with volunteers should gain from a general review of some of the issues that local volunteers are facing in carrying out the international exchange programs their organizations sponsor.

The book is divided into three parts. Part I: Managing Your Organization: Leadership, Purpose, Planning, and Structure, examines the basic components of organizational life. Organizations are created for a purpose, which must be articulated in a way that is convincing both for the volunteers you seek to recruit as well as for the financial support you hope to raise. Organizations need planning if they are to be effective. I have attempted to present a simple planning process that contains the major elements of much of the writing on this subject.

Leading and organizing are the other two components of managing your organization. There must be a structure within which people have clearly assigned responsibilities. As volunteers in international exchange today, we operate in many different organizational forms on community, national, and international levels. I will try to describe each of these and note how different organizational structures meet different needs. If you are a local volunteer for your Council for International Visitors or for Sister Cities, you will obviously be in a different relationship with your organization than if you are a chapter president for AFS.

Most important, however, one must understand that there is a difference between management and leadership. Leadership can be the most challenging and demanding of all requirements in managing your local exchange effort. The basic difference between the two is that *management* is a series of activities aimed at efficiently carrying out an organization's purpose, while *leadership* involves the articulation of purpose and vision and the coordination of people and other resources in a way that represents the values and ethics of those who choose to work for your cause. For this reason, I have started the book with a description of some of the things you can do to enable you to become not just a manager, but a leader of your local effort.

In Part II: Managing Your Resources: People, Programs, and Finances, I have outlined the three basic areas on which you need to keep an eye in order to ensure that the organization is operating effectively: your people, your products, and your money. This is perhaps even more true of volunteer organizations, since volunteer patterns have changed so dramatically over the last twenty years. Part II will examine some of these changes in volunteer motivation and the effect these have had on the way in which you must recruit and motivate today.

Part III: Managing the Cross-Cultural Experience: Culture Shock, Counseling, and Global Education, is the most specialized section of the book; it deals specifically with questions that affect the youth exchange field. If you are not involved in long-term youth exchange work, bringing students to the United States for a year in high school or supporting foreign students at American colleges and universities, you may only want to skim this part of the book. Those of you involved in the counseling and support of longer-term visitors, however, will find information unavailable in the general volunteer management literature.

Part IV: Managing Renewal: Of Yourself, Your Organization, and Others, closes this guide with an appeal to stop occasionally and "smell the flowers." Too many volunteers today are putting themselves under pressure to run from one activity to another without allowing time to take stock of themselves, their organizations, or the people with whom they work. The hope is that this chapter will provide some insight on the need for and benefits of this important part of volunteer leadership.

The diagram on effective volunteer management in Figure 1 presents the basic elements I have just described in a visual format. From time to time you may want to refer to it so as to remind yourself how managing your organization, your resources, and the exchange experience fit together.

Many of the ideas and suggestions in this book are based upon my own experience as a student participant, volunteer, host parent, and president of the American Field Service international student exchange organization, or AFS International/Intercultural Programs, as it is known today. These experiences have been supplemented by additional responsibility in the business world as president and chief operating officer of Holland America Cruises, an international passenger shipping company, and president of Moran, Stahl and Boyer, a New York management consulting firm specializing in assisting business corporations relocate their people and operations from one part of the country to another. My current work as a consultant to organizations from the United Nations system and Fortune 500 multinationals to small for-profit and not-for-profit organizations has underscored my conviction that many ideas about leadership contained in this book are applicable in a broad range of situations.

I would like to express my deep appreciation to the staff and volunteers of AFS, both in the United States and in the sixty countries around the world where AFS has program operations. They gave me my first opportunity to discover the challenge of bringing the rich variety of the world's people and cultures together to accomplish common purposes. I would also like to thank the Dutch officers and Indonesian and Filipino crew of the Holland America ships who reconfirmed my belief that people in both for-profit and not-for-profit organizations respond to openness and the sharing of information by demonstrating a willingness to accept additional responsibility and work toward common purposes.

Finally, writing a book is never possible without the direct support and encouragement of family, friends, and colleagues. I would like to take this opportunity first of all to thank my family—my wife, Kathe,

Figure 1

A Leadership Model for International Exchange Programs

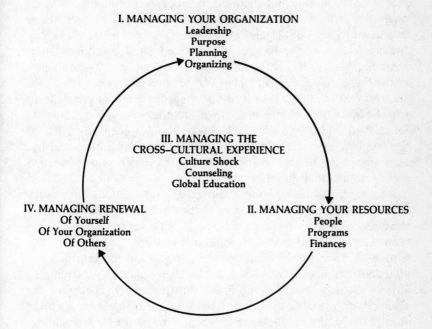

I. MANAGING YOUR ORGANIZATION
Leadership
Purpose
Planning
Organizing

III. MANAGING THE
CROSS–CULTURAL EXPERIENCE
Culture Shock
Counseling
Global Education

IV. MANAGING RENEWAL
Of Yourself
Of Your Organization
Of Others

II. MANAGING YOUR RESOURCES
People
Programs
Finances

my sons, Christopher and Colin, and our current AFS daughter from Australia, Lisa Dixon, for their patience and willingness to let me spend holidays and weekends working on this guide.

I am grateful to the United States Information Agency, which has kept me involved in international exchanges after I thought I had "retired." To Charles Wick, the director, who has given me extraordinary opportunities to participate in the President's International Youth Exchange Initiative. To Donna Oglesby, Director of the Youth Exchange Office, for whom this guide was rewritten, I want to express my particular appreciation.

The colleagueship and encouragement of the presidents and chief operating officers of many exchange organizations has also been important to me—Bill Dyal of AFS, Tom Gittins of Sister Cities, Jay Niemczyk of People-to-People, John Richardson of Youth for Understanding, Alan Rubin of the Partners of the Americas, Wayne Smith of the Friendship Force, and Alan Warne of the National Council for International Visitors. I want to add a special word of gratitude to Charlie MacCormack, the innovative and prescient president of The Experiment in International Living, who has ever been supportive of my continued presence in the international exchange field and has encouraged me to remain involved on numerous occasions when I was drawn in other directions.

Many professionals in these and other organizations have taken time to reread the first edition of *Bring Home the World* and have provided extremely helpful guidance for this second edition. I am particularly grateful to Dave Hoopes of The Intercultural Press, Neal Grove of AFS, Bob Sprinkle of the Association for International Practical Training, Karen Kale of The Experiment in International Living, George Brown of the Friendship Force, Joe Hickey of the Council for International Educational Exchange, and Dave Bachner, Robbins Hopkins and Deborah Dokken of Youth for Understanding.

All of these people have been good teachers and advisors and in this book I have attempted to pass along some of what I have learned from them. If I have been unsuccessful, it is a personal failure and not in any way that of the dedicated and talented people in the organizations with which I have worked.

Stephen H. Rhinesmith
Pelham Manor, New York
April, 1985

Bring Home the World

Part I:

MANAGING YOUR ORGANIZATION: LEADERSHIP, PURPOSE, PLANNING, AND STRUCTURE

Leadership: The Soul of Management

Writing a management guide for volunteers is a dangerous business. Many volunteers I know have told me they feel that management is somehow "dehumanizing" and that people who consider themselves good managers don't really "care about people."

I have found the reverse to be true. People who are good managers and respected leaders care very deeply about the people with whom they work. This is the reason they are eager to understand management techniques and practices that will enable people to work together in a smooth and cooperative way and to gain a sense of satisfaction and accomplishment from their activities.

SOME PERSONAL LEARNINGS ABOUT PURPOSE AND SOUL

The capacity to manage and lead others successfully is intimately related to our personal sense of self-worth and our general attitude toward others. If we feel good about ourselves, we will be able to work with others to help them build upon their strengths and compensate for their weaknesses. If we are threatened by those strengths, or intolerant of weaknesses, it lessens our ability to bring people together for the common good.

Another quality to which people respond is a sense of "soul." Soul is difficult to describe. It is the ability to make people feel good about themselves and their activities and at the same time help them see the relationship between their own activities and a higher purpose—one valued by society as a whole. In other words, it is identifying a sense of mission for your organization and maintaining a communication with your volunteers that makes them want to work with you.

Brian O'Connell, President of the Independent Sector, an advocacy organization for the volunteer sector of the United States, writes in his book, *Effective Leadership in Voluntary Organizations,* that:

> People who get involved with public causes often open
> themselves to frustration and disappointment, but—through
> it all and after it all—those moments of making change
> happen for the better are among their lasting joys. There's
> something wonderfully rewarding in being part of an effort
> that does make a difference. And there's something sparkling
> about being among other people when they're at their best.[1]

Creating the sparkle is something volunteer leaders with soul accomplish. They enable people to be their best in working for an effort that does make a difference.

It is interesting that most leaders who can effectively translate meaning into organizational life also display these values in their interpersonal dealings. I would like to share with you some simple lessons which the well-known psychologist, Carl R. Rogers, has found important for him in working with people.[2] After each I will recount for you my own experience in applying these learnings. These ideas are not in any order of importance, but are all of constant significance for me in living and working with people whether in my personal, professional, or volunteer life.

> Lesson 1: "In my relationship with persons I have found that
> it does not help, in the long run, to act as though I was some-
> thing that I am not."

Openness and candor about problems and a willingness to accept one's own strengths and weaknesses are qualities most volunteers appreciate in a leader. When I don't know something, I try to admit it; when I need help, I try to ask for it. I say "try," because I know from experience that this is not always easy. In some cases it has placed me in an awkward position. If we are working in a volunteer effort to increase understanding among peoples from different countries, however, I believe that we are called upon to reflect these same qualities in the way in which we deal with one another within our own organization.

If our purpose is to encourage international dialogue, we must be open to dialogue with one another. If our purpose is to encourage fuller understanding and tolerance of differences internationally, we must be understanding of differences among ourselves and demonstrate a tolerance and willingness to accept one another within our own community. If we encourage our international visitors to care about people they meet and develop relationships of mutual trust and confidence, we must develop the same sort of relationships with one another so as to facilitate the way we work together in our programs. If we believe participants in our programs should seek a better understanding of themselves, then we also must seek a better understanding and acceptance of ourselves; part of that process is to be open to others who seek to help us know ourselves more fully.

These are not easy standards to live by. But they are the ideals and standards we have set for those who participate in our programs, and as leaders in such programs we have a responsibility to be models of such behavior. It is to everyone's benefit.

Lesson 2: "I find I am more effective when I can listen acceptantly to myself and can be myself."

A leader must first be able to lead himself or herself;[3] she must listen to the small inner voices that speak of happiness for work done well or disappointment for work poorly done.

She must also listen "acceptantly," so as to recognize her own limitations and her needs for help. It is a well-known psychological phenomenon that people find it difficult to accept in others that which they cannot accept in themselves. If we are to be at peace with others, then we must strive to be at peace with ourselves.

One of the most wonderful stories about self-acceptance was contained in a paper entitled "Mellowing: An Alternative to Coping" by Dr. Darold A. Treffert, a psychiatrist who was chairman of the State Medical Society of Wisconsin. He relates how he learned the best definition of self-esteem and self-acceptance from his youngest son, Jay Jay.

I call him "Old 42" because he is always wearing that same tired sweat shirt around the house with the number 42 on it.

Every night at 9 o'clock Jay Jay, all those years I have been privileged to live with the little guy, comes into my study to say goodnight. He has always said, and continues to say in a predictable litany, "Goodnight, Dad. See you in the morning. Sweet dreams, I love you." Sometimes I put my arm around Old Number 42 and say something like "Jay Jay, old friend, old pal, old buddy of mine, you are a neat little guy. I love you very much. You are a special person. In fact, I think you are one of the neatest and nicest people on the whole planet." Jay Jay always modestly says—"I know."[4]

That's self-esteem!

In your leadership of others, it is important to be able to say "I know" to yourself once in a while when people say you have been thoughtful or helpful, or have done something well. And you also need to help others accept themselves in a similar way.

Over the years, there has been an odd incongruence between volunteers' work and their willingness to accept praise and thanks for a job well done. Indeed, many women today are struggling to acknowledge to themselves that all the work they have done as "just volunteers" has real value in the marketplace, that building on the skills they gained as volunteers enables them to start new careers which can bring new satisfactions.

As a volunteer leader, it is therefore important "to know" and to help others "to know" they are special and that it's all right to believe it and acknowledge it to themselves and others.

Lesson 3: "I have found it of enormous value when I can permit myself to understand another person."

Permitting oneself to understand another person, as Rogers describes it, involves a conscious effort to go beyond our initial judgments of people and be open to finding out who they really are.

How many times have you met foreign visitors and wondered how you would get through an evening, week, month, or year with them? Our initial reactions to differences are often negative. Yet how many times have these same people opened wonderful new opportunities for learning about the world and yourself—if you let yourself be open to understanding them and communicating with them.

Our willingness and ability to suspend initial predispositions and judgments will give us rich surprises in our dealings with people from other countries, as well as our relationships with other volunteers in our own community.

Lesson 4: "I have found it enriching to open channels whereby others can communicate their feelings, their private perceptual world to me."

It is strange how often we think of "international understanding" as a process of other people understanding one another. The first step toward international understanding, however, is for me to open channels that let people communicate their ideas and feelings about me and my country to me. This is difficult, since sometimes it hurts me to hear what they have to say and I want to close them out.

It seems that there are many people in the world running around looking for people whom they can help to gain international understanding, but who run right by those they are searching for. This happens because they don't listen to people or communicate with them. If they did, they'd find that most people are quite willing to share their ideas. It is only our limited openness that prevents us from hearing and understanding what they have to say.

Lesson 5: "I have found it highly rewarding when I can accept another person."

True acceptance of another person is not easy. Acceptance means not only *understanding* that someone holds a different set of perceptions and beliefs, but *accepting* these as valid for the other person if not for you.

This is of course most difficult when the other person's beliefs conflict directly with ours and threaten us. In working with a wide range of personalities around the world, we often have disagreements in values, philosophies, and behavior. When this happens to me, I try to understand why I am threatened and what there is about their beliefs that provide them with a sense of comfort and security. When I begin to get down to the reason people feel one way or another or see life from a different perspective, then I can truly move toward accepting them.

When direct conflict occurs because I and the other person are both trying to dominate a situation by imposing our own value system, I get as frustrated and angry as anyone else. But I try to see it as a disagreement over the issue and not denigrate the other person's character just because he or she may feel differently from the way I do.

> Lesson 6: "The more I am open to the realities in me and in the other person, the less do I find myself wishing to rush in and 'fix things.'"

As I listen to myself and sense what is going on inside me, I try to extend the same listening attitude to other people. The more I understand why they feel and think the way they do, the less compelled I am to rush in and try to change them in some way.

This patience is particularly important in counseling foreign students who may be having difficulty adjusting to cultural assumptions and values they find here in the United States. My tendency has sometimes been to wish I could straighten out their thinking and make them understand that they are wrong.

The fact is, they are not wrong—they are different. And the sooner I learn that the better!

There is another way that one tries to "fix things"—trying to "help" people. We sometimes see people as needing help when they do not want nor need it. Rushing in to help people prematurely can create frustration and resentment. It can also result in their becoming overly dependent.

In counseling students and working with colleagues, it is therefore important to sit back and ask yourself whether this person really needs your help, or whether you are rushing in to fix things, because you have a need to be needed or are threatened by what they are doing or thinking.

> Lesson 7: "What is most personal is most general."

Finally, I have found that the things I feel are most personal are those that, many times, are shared by other people. In fact, that is one of the reasons I try to express my feelings of the moment, especially when speaking to groups. If you sense what a group is feeling and articulate it, there is an identification in the room that can be truly inspiring. Inspiration is not in words or ideas, it is in the relevance of these ideas to the people who hear them. When a group hears something they deeply feel collectively, but have been unable to put into words, it can be a very motivating experience. This is one of the reasons why the articulation of "purpose" is such a critical part of leadership.

And so we come full circle to the "vision" upon which people build their commitment to causes and organizations. The goal of a world community in which people understand one another, care about one another, and are willing to work together to solve common difficulties in an open, cooperative, and effective manner will probably never be realized. But it is a goal that seems to be shared by many people throughout the world. When this dream is expressed, and an organizational opportunity to work toward it is provided, many people are invariably inspired to try to bring about its realization.

IMPLICATIONS FOR LEADERSHIP

These lessons have been important to the relationships I have had with people in many parts of the world during the last twenty-five years during which I have worked internationally. They have also been important in helping me discharge the responsibilities I have had for managing and guiding others toward productive, cooperative endeavor. As such they have formed the basis for a philosophy and style of leadership that I have found personally rewarding and organizationally effective.

In terms of leadership, these values can be translated into the following five basic guidelines:

1. You are leading most effectively when you help the people around you become strong and competent in their own work.

2. Leadership is best established when you can build relationships of trust with the people who choose to work with you.

3. A great deal of the function called leadership is structuring cooperative relationships among people who can themselves do the work that needs to be done.

4. It is important to confront conflicts that develop either between yourself and others, or between others, in a way that is direct

but supportive and encourages the containment and resolution of those conflicts.

5. Organizational leadership is heavily dependent upon the
    leader's ability to stimulate people to work together toward a
    common goal within a common purpose.

This last concern for organizational purpose and goals takes us to
the beginning point in our volunteer management tasks—a review of
the purposes of international exchange.

For Further Study

Miller, Lawrence M. *American Spirit: Visions of a New Corporate Culture.* New York:
    William Morrow and Company, 1984.
O'Connell, Brian. *Effective Leadership in Voluntary Organizations.* New York: Walker
    and Company, 1981.
Pascarella, Perry. *The New Achievers: Creating a Modern Work Ethic.* New York: The
    Free Press, 1984.
Rogers, Carl. *On Becoming a Person.* New York: Houghton-Mifflin, 1961.

The Purposes of International Exchange

You may not have thought about it before, but you are part of a national, indeed an international, movement of people throughout the world who share a common identity, common beliefs, and common aspirations. It is important to understand these bonds and to be able to articulate them to your local volunteers as you seek to attract people and financial resources for your organization's activities.

THE PURPOSES OF INTERNATIONAL EXCHANGE

The international exchange movement in the United States today encompasses a significant range and breadth of people. Community exchange organizations exist in every state and the major national youth exchange organizations claim local chapters which, when combined, touch over 4,000 U.S. communities. In addition, hundreds of thousands of volunteers in the YMCA, Rotary, the Girl Scouts, and Boy Scouts are also involved in international exchanges sponsored by these organizations as part of their general program activities. It is estimated that over 1,000,000 Americans are involved annually as members of host families alone![1]

The ideals and purposes that drive these volunteers reflect the hopes and dreams of the organizations for which they work. When we examine these, we discover that the international exchange community has never been short on purpose. We started with the idea of increasing international understanding as a means of maintaining peace in the world and went on from there!

Senator Fulbright reflected on this in a recent speech before the Council on International Educational Exchange, noting:

> Perhaps the greatest power of educational exchange is the power to convert nations into peoples and to translate ideologies into human aspirations. I do not think educational exchange is certain to produce affection between peoples, nor indeed do I think that it is one of its necessary purposes; it is quite enough if it contributes to the feeling of a common humanity, to an emotional awareness that other countries are populated not by doctrines that we fear but by individual people—people with the same capacity for pleasure and pain, for cruelty and kindness, as the people we were brought up with in our own countries.[2]

Senator Fulbright's remarks reflect an overriding theme of the 1950s. International exchanges grew in the post-war era as a means to help people around the world readjust the distorted images of one another, which had been created by years of war. Increased international understanding and the maintenance of peace was and is today a significant force behind the international exchange movement. I am convinced that exchange experiences have inspired people of all ages to work together in universally beneficial international projects.

None of us, however, would want the success of international exchanges to be judged solely on the absence of armed conflict in the world. Indeed, the purpose of international exchanges has broadened over the last forty years to include not only international understanding, but also more concrete and specific objectives concerned with social and economic development, the transfer of technology, and the acquisition of the knowledge and skills necessary to improve the quality of life on a global level.

This diversification of the purposes of international exchange has been reflected in the diversity of organizations within the international exchange community. The traditional community-based youth exchange organizations, such as AFS International/Intercultural Programs, The Experiment in International Living, Rotary, and Youth for Understanding have increasingly been joined by other organizations offering more work-related exchanges. Two organizations that have led the way in this diversification are the International Association for the Exchange of Students for Technical Experience (IAESTE), which arranges exchanges for young people interested in technical work opportunities in other countries and AIESEC (in English, The International Association of Students in Economics and Business Management), which arranges management work experiences for college-age students in other countries.

At the same time that the exchange community has broadened its purpose, it has also broadened its age range. Organizations like People-to-People, Sister Cities, Partners of the Americas, the National Council for International Visitors and, most recently, The Friendship Force are offering people of all ages an opportunity to travel abroad, meet people in their homes, and establish relationships that "turn places into people."

As a result, the international exchange movement over the last twenty years has developed a number of purposes that have given identity to the organizations working to accomplish them, and has provided new meaning to the individuals who volunteer their time, energy, and talent in pursuit of these programs.

The four major purposes served by international exchanges in the United States today are:

1. *International understanding for the maintenance of international peace.* This is the underlying ideal motivating many people to volunteer for and participate in international exchanges.

2. *Acquisition of knowledge and skills.* This has been traditionally associated with formal educational experiences in which exchange students have traveled abroad to learn about another country's language, history, and culture or to acquire specialized technical skills unavailable in their own country.

3. *Transfer of technology and professional expertise.* Many exchange organizations and international professional associations founded in the last twenty years have become committed to sharing new advances in technology and professional disciplines on an international level. This has resulted in the development of international networks increasingly dedicated to improving the welfare of people on a global scale.

4. *Personal development.* It is clear that international travel serves to broaden individuals in many ways. Depending on the length and nature of the travel, these are some of the potential rewards:

an increased sense of self and self-confidence as a result of dealing successfully with unexpected situations.

a more informed global perspective on the interdependence of countries and the importance and nature of international politics and economics for everyone's future, regardless of professional responsibilities.

an increased sense of ease in taking risks necessary for continued personal and professional growth and development.

an increased level of tolerance and patience for the diversity of lifestyles, people, and approaches to dealing with basic human problems.

a serious career interest in the international arena, turning one's professional skills toward helping nations and peoples develop and utilize their resources to improve the quality of life throughout the world.

A description of organizations involved in sponsoring international exchanges is contained in the booklet, *One Friendship at a Time: Your Guide to International Youth Exchange,* published by the United States Information Agency as part of the President's International Youth Exchange Initiative. Copies can be obtained by writing Youth Exchange Consumer Information Center in Pueblo, Colorado. (Appendix I of this volume contains the names and addresses of all organizations listed in this booklet.)

These four purposes—international understanding for the maintenance of peace, the acquisition of skills and knowledge, the transfer of technology and professional expertise and personal development— undergird the international exchange movement in the United States today.

More important, they provide the vision, inspiration, and reason that people volunteer on a local community level to host visitors from abroad, raise funds, and give their time, energy, and talents to international exchange organizations.

FROM PURPOSES TO MEANINGS

One definition of leadership offered recently suggests that it is the ability to "make meanings for people."

As a leader of an international exchange program on a local level, you should or be able to translate these four purposes into meaningful reasons why people in your community should support your organization and its programs. You can do this by enabling the people currently in your organization to translate these purposes into meanings of personal significance to them.

One of the ways to help your volunteers understand their ownership of the broader purposes of international exchange is to conduct this exercise with your committee members: Ask each person to examine the four purposes outlined above, and then write down which purposes are meaningful to them in working with your organization. In other words, what satisfaction or learning related to these purposes do they receive in their volunteer work? They should be as descriptive as possible in telling *how* these purposes have meaning for them.

Typical of the kinds of responses you might get are:

I have a feeling I am doing something to help people in the world understand one another better. It makes me feel good, especially when all I read about in the newspaper is violence and misunderstanding between people and nations. (Purpose 1)

I believe that the people who visit our community are getting an image of the *real* America, not the one they always see in the movies and the TV programs that are exported overseas. I feel like I am doing something to show the rest of the world that we are just like they are, with the same concerns, beliefs and desires that they have. (Purpose 2)

I have really enjoyed seeing the young people we have hosted learn new skills and become fluent in English. I believe that the hours I have spent tutoring exchange students in English will make a dramatic difference in their future. Their English fluency will give them professional opportunities that most other young people in their countries will not have. I feel like I have contributed significantly to improving the opportunity for a better life for someone else in the world. (Purpose 2)

I really enjoyed hosting the group of architects from Brazil last year. We had a great program planned for them and I am not sure who learned the most — they or the architects in our city. Some of the Brazilian architecture is really fantastic and I have had architects from our community calling me for more information about how they can maintain contacts. I am making as much of a contribution to the people of our community as I am to the Brazilians who were able to go home with new professional ideas and relationships. (Purpose 3)

I have gained a great deal personally from my work with foreign visitors. I have learned a lot of geography — who would ever know where Mbabane was if they hadn't had someone from Swaziland in their home for dinner? I feel more in touch with the world and my life is broader, richer and fuller than it was when the boundaries of my interests were this community, and maybe some state or national issues which affected our family. (Purpose 4)

I have seen the difference the chance to know foreign visitors has made for my kids. I feel I am giving them a view of the world that I never had when I was growing up. Can you imagine that we've had people from over fifteen countries in our home for dinner? The night after the visitor leaves, we sit down with our kids and talk about what we learned about the visitor and his or her country and lifestyle. (Purpose 4)

These are *meanings* — they translate into things that people *feel* they are doing that give them a sense of satisfaction, pleasure, and accomplishment. *Meanings are the personal side of purposes.*

When everyone in your group has completed this exercise, you can ask them to describe what they have discovered. You may find there are meanings in your organization you never thought of. These meanings are the reasons people volunteer. They are the perceived benefits of being involved in an effort that extends beyond oneself and one's personal or professional life.

While understanding and articulating your organization's purpose and meaning is important to you in your work with volunteers, these processes are equally important in fund-raising, publicity, and all the other activities you are engaged in on behalf of your organization. The clearer you are about your purposes and what fund-raising, publicity, and your programs mean to you, your community, and the world, the more effective you will be in achieving your program objectives. Let us now move on to examine the planning process and how you can use a clear sense of purpose to focus the allocation of your organizational resources toward those activities that will best enable you to meet your objectives.

For Further Study:

Coombs, Philip H. *The Fourth Dimension of Foreign Policy: Educational and Cultural Affairs.* New York: Harper & Row, 1964.

Fisher, Glen. *Public Diplomacy and the Behavioral Sciences.* Bloomington, Ind.: Indiana University Press, 1972.

Klineberg, Otto. *The Human Dimension in International Relations.* New York: Holt, Rinehart and Winston, 1966.

Rhinesmith, Stephen H. "Negotiating International Youth Exchange Agreements," Washington, D.C.: Youth Exchange Office, United States Information Agency, 1983.

Planning for Effectiveness

3

Planning has become a very popular activity today—everybody is doing it. Unfortunately, too much of that planning focuses only on operational details, with little concern for the ultimate outcome of a program or how it, in turn, is related to the overall purpose and direction of an organization.

In order to make sure this doesn't happen to you, you should "plan for effectiveness." In the following pages I want to share with you what this means and how you can do it.

PLANNING FOR EFFECTIVENESS

"Effectiveness" has been a popular management term ever since Peter Drucker wrote *The Effective Executive* in 1966. In that book Drucker defined effectiveness as "The art of concentrating on what is important rather than what is urgent."[1]

Over the years the distinction has also been made between "efficiency" and "effectiveness," with the former referring to the ratio between costs and benefits and the latter encompassing the dimensions of purpose, quality, and durability. In other words, you can be "efficient" in getting work done quickly and smoothly, but the end result may be something which does not fit within the overall purpose or values of your organization, lacks the quality which you stand for, or is a "quick-fix" for a longer-term need.

There are four questions which need to be answered for *effective* planning. These are:

1. What *needs* exist in your community that are *within your purpose*?

2. What *programs, goals, and activities* can you undertake to meet these needs?

3. What *priority-setting* do you need to do *in light of the resources* you have available?

4. How will you *evaluate your results* to know if you have been *successful* when your activities are completed?

These four questions translate into four basic tests: The Purpose Test; The Goal-setting Test; The Resources Test; and The Success Test. Let's look at each and see what it means for you in your annual planning process.

THE PURPOSE TEST

There are two starting points to planning—the *needs* of your community and the *purpose* of your organization. I have seen many dedicated volunteers go in the wrong direction by concentrating only on one or the other.

People who look only at the purpose of their organization when developing goals and activities may plan activities that are not needed by the community they serve. When you annually test the purposes of your organization against the needs of your community, you have a good test of whether your organization is still relevant to your community.

There are many examples of volunteer efforts that were started to meet certain needs of the community at one time and which continue today, not because they still meet those needs, but because they meet the needs of the people who volunteer for them!

NEEDS ASSESSMENT

The first place to start is with the needs of the people in your community. Do they need what your organization has to offer (for example, in the area of international high school and class exchange, and for adults, professional/cultural exchanges)? Have their needs changed since the last time you set your program priorities? What were the results of your last year's activities? What lessons can be learned from last year's experience that will make this year's goal-setting more successful?

Once you have identified the needs of your community in the international exchange area, there are two other needs which you must assess—the needs of your international visitors and your own needs.

How successful were you last year in meeting the needs of your international visitors? Were there areas that were weak? Why? Were there areas that were strong? Why? Has anything changed in the resources you have available for this year which will change this situation—either positively or negatively? If the reason something was weak or strong was not a question of the availability of people or funds, but rather of procedures and scheduling, will you be able to do this as well or better this year than you did in the past?

Finally, how about your own needs—are they being met? As we shall discuss in more depth in Chapter 5, all of us who volunteer have needs to be met. If our volunteer activity does not meet our needs, we will not continue to volunteer. It is therefore important to examine realistically whether your own needs and the needs of others in your group are being met by your current activities and organizational procedures.

PURPOSE ASSESSMENT

It is important, when assessing what community, international visitor, or personal needs are relevant for goal-setting, to make sure that these needs are still within your organization's purpose.

I have seen many dedicated volunteers, whose personal interests and needs have changed, try to redefine the purpose of an organization they deeply admire so that they can continue to work with that organization. One of the realizations we all must face as we mature is that few organizations can meet all the changing needs of a community or all of our own changing needs as volunteers. As a result, regardless of how much we have gained from our association with an organization in the past, we must realize that there comes a time for us to move on to other activities, rather than try to force something we have cared about into a direction that may not be best for its purpose, goals, and objectives.

On the other hand, it is obviously important to test the relevance of your organization's purpose to today's world. You may have to undertake new activities or programs in order to enable your group to meet future needs and not become obsolete. Differences of opinion over this matter are part of the core issues facing the policy-making bodies of most organizations—both profit and not-for-profit.

Since most local community organizations involved in international exchange are part of an international association of organizations dedicated toward the same purpose, there is somewhat less freedom to redefine the purposes of your local organization than if you were a totally local entity. The nature of international exchange work means that there must be a partner in another country who shares your purpose and priorities and is willing to work with you. This is difficult for a single community to establish with a variety of communities abroad. Central offices and international associations, therefore, provide this service. At the same time, one must pay the price of certain philosophical and operational constraints if one is to take advantage of the international contacts and operational convenience provided by an international coordinating body.

Indeed, this restraint on the flexibility to redefine your local organizational purpose and priorities without gaining approval from other parties in different cities and different parts of the world is a good test of your true interest in a world community! The concept of world community implies a merging of interests and a negotiation of individual concerns against the common good. The frustration we on a local level sometimes feel with national or international constraints is to a degree a test of our ability to work within one of the ultimate purposes of the international exchange movement—the interdependence of people in a world community.

In the Purpose Test, therefore, a balance must be struck between the needs of your community, the international visitors you serve, and your own needs on the one hand, and the purpose of your organization and the interdependent nature of international exchange work on the other. Not an easy exercise, but one which can be enormously stimulating and useful if examined periodically to ensure that all the people in your organization remain committed to the work you are doing, believe in its relevance, and are personally gaining from their continued association and responsibilities.

THE GOAL–SETTING TEST

After you have assessed the needs you want to meet during the next year and their relevance to your organization's mission and purpose, you are in a position to identify programs and goals you would like to accomplish and to determine specific activities to achieve these goals.

There is nothing mysterious about goal-setting. It is a simple process of deciding *what* you want to do, *how* you are going to do it, and *when* you would like to get there.

The best way to approach your program planning process is to ensure that you have conducted a "brainstorming" session on all the ways you can carry out your organization's mission and purpose. A brainstorming session is a fancy term to describe the process whereby you and your chapter members get together, with a blackboard or paper and pen handy, and state what you would like to do with your organization in the next year, *if resources were no constraint.*

During a brainstorming process, *no one can discuss or comment on the merit of someone else's idea*—there is to be no "red-lighting." Only "green-lighting," or encouraging people in their ideas, no matter how preposterous, is allowed. That may sound strange, but in this way people become stimulated by different ideas and provide modifications to "far-out" suggestions that can lead to exciting new realistic programs.

There has been a great deal of research on goal-setting from a psychological perspective as well as an organizational viewpoint. One study by David C. McClelland, which has gained widespread acclaim, notes that goals should have three basic characteristics.[2]

First, a goal should be *specific*. It should be something more than "to help people in our community understand the rest of the world." Instead, a specific program goal would be "to provide our international visitors with an understanding of our community through observation of life in a family, the social and economic structure of our community, and our local political process." This is a workable objective, of course, only if you have the time available to carry it out. We will talk further about the availability of resources in a few minutes.

Second, a goal should be *challenging but realistic*. It does little good to set a specific goal that cannot be attained. At the same time, it is not very stimulating to set organizational or personal goals that do not provide a challenge. One of the keys to motivating volunteers is to keep them challenged. When work becomes boring or routine, people lose interest and fade away.

Third, every goal should be *time-phased*—that is, a specific date should be designated for its achievement. Unless a date is attached to a goal, it is difficult to stimulate the kind of action necessary to attain it. For example, if you say that by July 1 you want to be ready to host a group of thirty Japanese businessmen in your community for a week, there will be a series of steps you need to take between now and then in order to make it happen.

This is called *action planning.* In the case of the visit by the Japanese businessmen, it means that by June 1 you will need to have your program of activities completely planned and that by June 15 all of your families will need to be recruited for home hospitality. Probably by June 20, advance publicity should begin in local newspapers in order to let people know that your visitors will be in town. And so the process goes on. In any case, such action planning is stimulated by setting a specific date by which you need to reach your goal and then thinking backward from that date to the present time in order to determine the sequence of activities that needs to be undertaken.

THE RESOURCES TEST

You can set all the goals you want, but if your plans are not backed up in the context of a *realistic availability of financial and human resources,* you might as well save yourself the time and effort of going through the first steps.

FINANCIAL RESOURCES

Today, as always, most volunteer organizations do not have enough money to do even half of what they would like to do. A realistic assessment of your financial resources is therefore one of the first and most important steps in your planning process. Once you have outlined your ideal set of programs and activities for the year ahead, you need to set priorities based upon the resources you think you will have available. If you are uncertain about the amount of financial resources you will have, you should set those programs you know you can fund, and then establish a plan and timetable for adding other programs should more funds become available.

On the other hand, your budget should not *control* your planning. Too many people *start* planning by looking at their budget. This puts an artificial constraint on thinking and tends to reinforce carrying on the same activities year after year. A needs-assessment, goal-setting process which examines creatively what it is you would *like* to do with your organization in the coming year can result in attracting additional funds to support new, exciting activities.

HUMAN RESOURCES

Even more important than money is people. Organizations are more constrained and enriched by the quality and commitment of their people than they are by technology, finances or any other force in the world. The right people with the right commitment can overcome almost any outside obstacle standing in the way of an organization's achieving its purpose.

Think for a minute about the truly exciting and successful ventures in which you have been involved. Were these successful only because they had enough money behind them? Or were they successful because they had the right talent and commitment applied in the right way against the right objectives? People truly *do* make the difference.

It is therefore critical that you objectively assess the availability, talent, and commitment of your people. Many times in volunteer organizations we fail in managing the necessary human resources because we are not realistic in assessing one of the following three keys.

People must be available

Much of volunteer work, especially in international exchange programs, involves having people available to assist in meeting visitors' needs and dealing with last-minute changes, which seem to inevitably occur. Obviously, if your people are not available when needed, you have a problem. Either you should not enter into your planned project or you need to recruit additional people. Avoid the temptation to plan to do it yourself! It never works in the long run and many times it doesn't work in the short run either, except at some cost to you or the project, which is usually not really best for anyone.

People must have the talents needed

A great number of volunteer projects fail because the wrong person was given the wrong responsibility for the wrong reason. Availability is not the main criterion to be applied to job assignments, but in volunteer organizations it often takes precedence over performance. This is one of the most difficult areas of volunteer organization leadership; it requires some hard thinking about what needs to be done and who can do it, and this may result at times in some hard decisions which require diplomatic action. The correct assessment and assignment of responsibilities is, however, one of the most important skills a leader needs to develop.

People must be committed

Availability and talent will be of little use without commitment. Commitment is the motivation that moves people to use their availability and talent for the relevant needs. It is obtained and maintained through leadership. We will talk more in Chapter 5 about recruiting and motivating the right volunteers for the right positions. At this point, let us point out that the development of commitment rests on the two factors we mentioned in Chapter 1: articulating the organization's purpose in a way that enables people to identify with it and developing a climate and procedures in the organization that show respect for the contributions that each individual can make.

Once you have completed testing the financial and human resources against your programs and determined the priorities you want to set as a result of the constraints and opportunities presented by these resources, your final step in the planning process is to apply the "success test."

THE SUCCESS TEST

The success test is basically a test to determine whether you have reached your objectives. It focuses on whether you have done what you set out to do. In order to accomplish this, your program goals should be *measurable*. This means that in addition to being specific, challenging, and time-phased, your goals should be quantifiable in a way that will allow you to know when you have attained them. Measuring achievement is very difficult in volunteer work and even more difficult in something as vague as "international understanding." Nevertheless, you should try to set some goals for yourself which can be measured in terms of the programs you are undertaking.

For example, in the case of the Japanese visitors mentioned earlier, you might say that during the time they are in your town, you would like to have five newspaper interviews for them, make sure they are covered by at least one television program, and try to expose them to at least four hundred local community people through home stays, an evening panel discussion, and a Saturday evening banquet. Furthermore, as a result of their being here, you would like to see at least ten new persons recruited to work with your club or committee next year. All of these become measurable goals by which you can determine the publicity generated by your hospitality.

It would be even better if these goals could be specified in terms of *final insights* you hope to provide for the people in your community and the Japanese visitors. In this case, you might consider that you will have obtained your goal if 75 percent of the people who kept the visitors in their homes could characterize their experience as positive, could describe five new perspectives they gained on Japanese life or on their own community, and would be willing to host another visitor the next time a group comes to town. This would be another measurable result from your activity.

Here, then, is the planning process for effectiveness. I hope you will share the key concepts with other members of your local organization and use this guide as you consider your program plans for the next year.

For Further Study

Connors, Tracy D. (Editor-in-Chief), *The Nonprofit Organization Handbook*. New York: McGraw-Hill Company, 1980.

Drucker, Peter F. *Managing for Results*. New York: Harper & Row, 1964.

Fisher, John. *How to Manage a Nonprofit Organization*. Toronto: Management and Fundraising Centre, Publishing Division, 1978.

Hughes, Charles L. *Goal Setting: Key to Individual and Organizational Effectiveness*. New York: American Management Association, 1965.

McConkey, Dale D. *MBO for Nonprofit Organizations.* New York: American Management Association, 1980.

Montana, Patrick J. and Diane Borst (eds.). *Managing Nonprofit Organizations.* New York: American Management Association, 1977.

Zaltman, Gerald (ed.). *Management Principles for Nonprofit Agencies and Organizations.* New York: American Management Association, 1981.

Organizing for Action

4

There are a wide variety of national and local organizational structures in the international exchange field. The three most prevalent are what we shall call the Association Model, the Chapter Model, and the Special Interest Model. Before we discuss details of your local organizational structure, it is important to understand the different national contexts within which you and other local volunteers operate in carrying out international exchange programs.

THE ASSOCIATION MODEL

Many organizations work on the Association Model. Some well-known national associations in the exchange field include the National Council for International Visitors, Sister Cities International (formally known as the Sister Cities Association), the National Association for Foreign Student Affairs, and the Council for International Educational Exchange.

While these organizations sponsor different kinds of exchange activities and serve differing clients, they are similar in structure: They are national associations of local committees, organizations, or individuals engaged in international exchange work. In such organizations, the local entities have a high degree of autonomy over their operations. They also determine their own programs and operate in ways that are supportive of the general purposes and framework of the national association, but they are not dependent upon the national organization for day-to-day guidance or operations.

In the Association Model, there is a national board of directors, comprised of elected representatives of local groups, who serve to oversee the general policies and directions of the organization. The national board also monitors the organization's relationship with other entities such as the U.S. government, national programming agencies, or other international exchange groups in this country and abroad.

In the National Association Model, there is an executive director or president who is the chief operating officer responsible for day-to-day coordination of the activities of the organization as a whole, representation of the organization with government and other private organizations, and preparation of accreditation procedures for new local groups wishing to join the association. The association staff is also responsible for planning and implementing an annual meeting of some kind to which all association members are invited.

In most cases, national associations have authority to sanction local organizations or individuals who do not adhere to general national guidelines. They also often support local organizations with small grants to assist them in projects that are within the national association's priorities.

The Association Model assumes a strong local organization with its own corporate structure, independent staff, and board of directors. The local organization pays dues to the national organization in return for membership activities, national and international representation, training, and general information dissemination.

THE CHAPTER MODEL

The Chapter Model has been the classic organizational pattern for the major youth exchange organizations like AFS and Youth for Understanding and for some adult exchange organizations like The Friendship Force and People-to-People International.

In such organizations local chapters carry out programs developed and designed by the national organization. They do not operate with autonomy, but within carefully prescribed procedures laid out by the parent organization. In most cases, these local chapters are not incorporated, but depend upon the national organization for their tax-deductibility, liability insurance, and legal framework for operations.

Chapters usually do not have paid staff nor even a "board" per se. Instead, the chapter often operates as a committee of the whole with different responsibilities assigned to specific individuals from year to year. There are no annual dues from the local organization to the national, but payments are made on a per capita basis for persons participating in exchange activities.

The parent organizations in most cases have large staffs and provide a great deal of day-to-day guidance and support of exchange program preparation and implementation. They have national or international boards of directors or trustees who oversee the policies and directions of the organization on a nonrepresentational basis. Many of these boards include persons not directly associated with the organization who provide particular expertise or access to financial and other resources.

In the Chapter Model, the parent organization works closely with national organizations in other countries to coordinate the sending and receiving of program participants. In youth exchange organizations in particular, local chapters seldom work directly with local chapters in other countries. In the adult organizations, however, relations between local committees in different countries are nationally sanctioned.

In most cases under the Chapter Model, national organizations raise or administer a central fund, which can be used to subsidize certain programs or worthy individuals nominated by chapters. National and regional training programs and other support services are also offered on an ongoing basis.

The Chapter Model assumes a strong national organization with local chapters comprised totally of volunteers. In most cases, local chapters will not be incorporated and will depend on the national organization for information, materials, applications, program procedures, travel coordination, and national and international representation.

THE SPECIAL INTEREST MODEL

A variation on the Chapter Model, the Special Interest Model is found in large national service associations like the YMCA/YWCA, Girl Scouts, Boy Scouts, Rotary, and other organizations whose primary purpose lies outside the exchange field. These organizations are involved in international exchanges, but as only one of many activities sponsored on a local level.

Special Interest Chapters also conform in some ways to the Association Model. From a national perspective, they operate very much like an association, with local groups having full autonomy over their operations and full determination of the kinds of activities in which they will participate. The role of the national organization is to provide information about exchange opportunities and arrange for contact between local chapters and chapters in other countries who would be interested in exchanges.

Special Interest Chapters usually operate without paid staff (in the case of local service organizations like Rotary), but in some cases may have such staff (as in the case of the YMCA and YWCA). National organizations publish general information and literature on the organization as a whole in which international activities are included, but there are few formally organized national activities directed toward training, developing, or supporting international exchange activities on a local level.

The Special Interest Model assumes that interested persons on the local level will take the initiative for starting and coordinating international activities within the overall framework of the organization. Most international exchanges are coordinated between chapters or committees in one country and counterparts in another country, with little interference or guidance from the parent organization.

OTHER ORGANIZATIONAL FORMS

Three other structural forms found in international exchanges represent the oldest and the newest, the easiest and most complex of all ways of operating. The oldest and easiest of these is individual representation and the newest and most complex are local, state, and national coalitions.

None of these has been included as a "model," because none represents an organizational form requiring the application of management principles for day-to-day operations. At the same time, it is important to acknowledge their existence, since organizations using these structural forms are playing increasingly important roles in international exchange in the United States.

INDIVIDUAL REPRESENTATIVES

Most of the for-profit exchange organizations, like the American Institute for Foreign Study, operate through individual representatives who recruit participants to go overseas and families to host persons coming from abroad. These organizations do not develop local volunteer groups, but instead depend upon their representatives to carry out "sales" activities within a highly prescribed product line.

Almost all not-for-profit organizations started this way. The individual who volunteers or is remunerated for developing exchange opportunities is still a major factor in international exchanges in the United States today. Since these persons are not involved in managing local volunteers, however, we have not concentrated on them in this guide.

LOCAL AND STATE COALITIONS

Over the years, there have been a variety of attempts to bring local community exchange groups together in coalitions to enhance their common interests. This has been a difficult task, since there is strong competition in many local communities for scarce resources like host families, students, and financial support.

Community coalitions have, however, been more successful in the global education movement, which we shall discuss more fully in Chapter 12. Global education is an effort among educators to increase the amount of attention given to "global issues" in elementary and secondary education. It is not an attempt to substitute "international affairs" for social studies in the curriculum, but instead is a drive to include an "international perspective" on subjects already taught. Thus, for example, in teaching mathematical concepts, their origin in ancient Egypt would be stressed, with some description about life in Egypt during those times and how mathematical ideas contributed to the culture.

The movement to "internationalize" school curricula has been led during recent years by Global Perspectives in Education. This organization has operated on national, state, and local levels to train teachers and orient educational administrators to the benefits and techniques of making school curricula more international. The effort by Global Perspectives in Education has been more successful than the international exchange movement in creating local coalitions of interested parties and has recently attracted considerable support from such prestigious sources as the Rockefeller and Danforth Foundations.

Nevertheless, with recent encouragement from the U.S. Information Agency, approximately twenty local, regional, and state coalition organizations have been developed in support of international exchange. These groups are endeavoring to find ways to cooperate across various special interests to stimulate a greater degree of support for international exchanges in general. This has resulted in expanded publicity and in some cases joint participation in recruiting and orientation.

The Partners of the Americas, operating on a state level with countries in Latin America, has long advocated the creation of State Councils for International Education, Exchange and Commerce. These councils would bring together the educational, exchange, and commercial interests in a state to sponsor ways of increasing citizen interest and support for international activities involving the state. There is growing interest in this effort and some of the coalition movements are particularly aimed at this level of opportunity.

NATIONAL COALITIONS

Beginning in the early 1980s, interest developed among parent organizations and associations involved in international exchange to find ways of information-sharing and exchange on a national level.

In 1980, in response to concerns about the coordination of the exchange during the future, the Consortium for International Citizen Exchange was formed. It was an influential group, comprised originally of the presidents of the eight major community-based exchange organizations—AFS, The Experiment in International Living, Friendship Force, National Council for International Visitors, Partners of the Americas, People-to-People International, Sister Cities International, and Youth for Understanding.

The presidents of these organizations met quarterly to discuss areas of mutual interest and to determine ways in which the public's awareness of international exchange could be enhanced within the United States.

The creation of this organization, however, resulted in several other national coalitions being formed for similar purposes. Since this gave rise to potential fragmentation of the field, rather than consolidation and cooperation, representatives of thirty-two organizations engaged in the President's International Youth Exchange Initiative agreed to gather at The Experiment in International Living in Brattleboro, Vermont, January of 1985, to determine whether common interests could better be served by the creation of some form of national association of international exchange organizations. At that meeting, tentative agreement was reached that such an organization would be useful, and steps are underway at the time of this writing to form such a coalition.

With such a wide range of organizational structures, it is obvious that community leaders in international exchange will have differing needs in determining what management principles are most appropriate to their organization. In this chapter and in this book generally, I have tended to concentrate on the Chapter Model, since persons operating within this structure are primarily on their own, without the benefit of local professional staff.

With this overview of organizational structures in the exchange field, we are now ready to turn to an examination of management principles affecting local organizational operations.

THREE BASIC PRINCIPLES OF ORGANIZATION

Chester I. Barnard, one of the first management theorists, wrote that "an organization is a system of cooperative human activities . . . "[1] If your experience in local volunteer organizations has been anything like mine, I imagine you have occasionally wondered how "cooperation" became synonymous with "organization"!

Well, the fact is that if there is no cooperation, there is no organization. To stimulate cooperation people must have positions which (1) meet the needs of the organization in a well-defined way; (2) are specific in their own right, with adequate descriptions of their responsibilities so that everyone understands what each job requires; and (3) meet the needs of the individuals who fill them. If you achieve all this in organizing your group, you will have one essential ingredient of an effective, enjoyable volunteer experience.

Since you probably review goals and programs annually, you should also review at that time your committee's structure to determine whether the jobs you have are adequate for your new goals during the coming year. Too many people continue with the same structure year after year, trying to perform new activities in an outmoded committee framework. In this guide, we are considering how you organize people *after* the planning process, precisely because the allocation of jobs and responsibilities should flow from the activities you have planned.

GENERAL COMMITTEE ORGANIZATION

Most volunteer groups in your community, regardless of national affiliation, probably have the traditional offices of president, vice-president, secretary, and treasurer, plus additional specialized roles depending upon the specific purpose and functions performed. The four positions noted, however, tend to represent ongoing functions necessary for planning and implementing *any* activities. Let us briefly consider each of these key responsibilities.

In general, the president is responsible for representation of the organization in the community as well as the leadership of chapter members. She is also responsible for financial and program planning.

The vice-presidential role is one that has been widely debated — from the national level of our government on down to the smallest local volunteer group. In most volunteer committees, however, vice-presidents tend to have a "program" function; they either coordinate the planning of meetings on a month-to-month basis or plan the general program for the year. In other instances, the vice-president may serve as the "alter-ego" to the president in a training capacity for succession to the presidency. In larger groups, the vice-president can often play a useful operating role as "executive director," freeing the president for fund-raising, speaking, and other representational activities, which allow the organization to become better known in the community.

The secretary's job is sometimes combined with the treasurer's. This is generally not a good idea. A secretary normally takes minutes and for this purpose must be able to identify and summarize major issues and decisions and express them clearly in writing. This is an important function in enabling a group to know what it has decided and allowing it to check at a later point whether it has accomplished what it said it would do.

The treasurer, on the other hand, must understand basic accounting principles and in many volunteer organizations is also the person responsible for fund-raising activities. For this reason, her functions

are very different from those of the secretary and need to be filled
by a person with different skills and interests. A basic ability with
figures and skill in preparing budgets and demonstrating the relationship between budgets, programs, and fund-raising objectives and
activities is extremely useful. When all these responsibilities are
combined, they require considerable organizational and leadership
talents.

Specialized jobs may be added if the nature of your group requires
them. Most international exchange committees have a "home hospitality coordinator" responsible for developing and maintaining a group
of families willing to host foreign visitors for a few days, a week or
two, or even a year. Most hospitality groups also have a "transportation
coordinator" responsible for identifying and maintaining a group of
volunteer drivers. These are needed to shuttle foreign visitors around
the community for activities from sightseeing to shopping. Other
roles may be necessary, depending upon the size, scope, and nature of
your committee's activities.

The job of "publicity coordinator" should also be standard in any
volunteer group, but is unfortunately often overlooked. With increasing competition among volunteer organizations for financial and
human resources, it is important that your group establish a clear
identity in order to attract new volunteers and to lay an adequate
groundwork for fund-raising. *There is nothing more difficult than
trying to raise funds for an organization that is unknown and whose
objectives are unclear.* It is the responsibility of the publicity coordinator to ensure that your community is aware of and appreciates your
group's goals and activities.

DEVELOPING AND USING JOB DESCRIPTIONS

Your immediate reaction to the use of job descriptions in volunteer
work may be that they are unnecessary and overly cumbersome.
"After all, this is just a volunteer group," you may say.

In very small groups, formal job descriptions may indeed be
unnecessary. However, once you are working with more than ten
people, job descriptions can be extremely helpful. They may even
become more important if there is high mobility in your membership,
with many people shifting in and out from year to year.

It is important to recognize that the management of voluntary organizations must be taken just as seriously as the management of profit-making organizations. And one of the basic principles that has evolved from the management of profit-making organizations is the value of a clear and concise job description. It strengthens motivation, performance, and evaluation—not to mention the added advantages that accrue when everybody knows what everybody else does!

Job descriptions should outline job tasks, as in the sample for a chapter president shown in Figure 2. At the end of each job description, there should be a list of the general qualifications and specific skills required for the position. This will make recruiting easier and allow persons being recruited to better judge their ability to carry out the job responsibilities.

If you do not have job descriptions for the key responsibilities in your local organization, I would suggest you try drafting some today. You may be surprised at what you will learn about your organization's structure and how it works (or doesn't work!).

THE ROLE OF THE BOARD OF DIRECTORS

As noted earlier, depending on your national affiliation, your group may or may not have a formal board of directors. If the organization is incorporated, it *must* have a board of directors to meet your legal obligations. If, however, your group follows the Chapter Model, you probably will not need a board. (In this case, you may want to skip to the next section of this chapter.)

Regardless of the variety of a board's composition and the size of the organization, any board of directors has certain basic duties. These duties follow from the organizational functions that make a board necessary. The six primary functions of a board are to:

1. establish the purpose and direction of the organization

2. review program plans and budgets

3. evaluate organizational effectiveness against purpose and objectives

4. evaluate the top administrator and select a new person for this role when necessary

Figure 2

Sample Job Description

Position: President, Hometown International Chapter

Responsible to: Board of Directors, Area (Regional, National Committee)

Tasks (Internal)

1. Develop and articulate mission, goals, and objectives for the chapter and establish programs, policies, procedures, and budget necessary for their achievement.
2. Organize volunteers in a structure which enables the chapter to carry out its mission and goals.
3. Establish procedures for recruiting and selecting people for chapter membership and develop programs for their orientation and training.
4. Inspire volunteers toward action aimed at realizing chapter goals through delegation of authority and responsibility and determination of accountability.
5. Conduct periodic evaluations of programs, structure, and membership to determine changes necessary.

Tasks (External)

1. Communicate the mission, programs, and goals of the chapter to participants, volunteers, and the public in a way which will motivate them to support the chapter.
2. Coordinate and personally solicit funds for support of programs and activities.
3. Consult with Board of Directors or membership in planning and make periodic reports on progress toward achieving organizational goals.

Special Knowledge and Skills Required

The presidency requires, first, an ability to work with people from many cultures, age groups, and backgrounds. Second, an ability to communicate, orally and in writing, so as to inspire persons to work for the organization. And, third, an ability to manage one's own time and the time of others in an efficient, effective, and focused manner.

---

5. represent the public need and interest to the organization

6. represent the organization to the public, especially to the sources of financial support[2]

These responsibilities are the same for all organizations. If they are not carried out by a board, then they must be carried out by committee members. If you do not have a board for your chapter or committee, you should ask yourself who is carrying out these important organizational tasks and be sure that each one is adequately covered.

CHARACTERISTICS OF BOARD BEHAVIOR

Karl Mathiasen III, of the Center for Community Change in Washington, D.C., has worked with a wide range of boards in a variety of organizations throughout the United States. In a small paper entitled "No Board of Directors Is Like Any Other: Some Maxims About Boards"[3] he makes a series of sometimes tongue-in-cheek, but very wise observations about board behavior. I have summarized these, adding some thoughts based on my own experience.

1. *Boards of directors generally have no memory worth mentioning;* it is a fact of life that volunteer, very part-time boards of directors do not remember well what happened at the last meeting, much less what they agreed to do several months ago.

2. *Boards of directors normally do not read;* if a staff's solution to a board's lapses of memory is to provide more and more material, then the agency is in real trouble.

3. *Staffs think that their boards "must" know more and do more than they will actually know or do;* to correct this, staffs should avoid building large agendas and concentrate on important matters of policy, principle, or direction.

4. *There is no right time to bring a new policy or new program to the board; it is always too early or too late;* a good committee structure can help to determine when and how to bring new policies and programs to the full board.

5. *It is a myth that boards make policies and staffs carry them out.* No board should "make policy" without deep involvement by the staff, usually as initiator, and always as co-equal in the decision-making process.

6. *The two most important people in any nonprofit organization are the executive director or president and the board chair; if one or the other is weak, so probably is the organization;* a balance of power, mutual respect, and basic agreement about long-term strategy and directions is essential for the fullest benefits from these two important roles.

7. *By-laws ought to be very general in nature; but they should always include a provision for rotation of board members;* every board needs new blood just as much as it needs the opportunity to gracefully thank old-timers for their participation; while requested retirement of board members is never easy, it is easier with a rotation policy than without.

8. *The most important board committee is the Nominating Committee;* it is responsible not only for nomination, but also for orienting new members, monitoring their contributions, determining their renomination, and communicating decisions not to renominate.

9. *A formal board orientation is a necessary part of every board member's effective work;* basic beliefs and directions of the organization must be fully understood and expectations concerning attendance, contribution, and performance should be outlined as specifically as possible.

10. *Boards do not raise money unless they raise it for themselves;* board members must be excited about the programs of the organization and feel "ownership" in having them financially supported.

11. *In the not-for-profit world there will always be some tension between the board and the staff;* staff specialists and volunteer generalists will always have different perspectives and sometimes different interests—that's what it's all about.

12. *A board's behavior often reflects where the organization is in terms of its age and growth;* organizing boards are often small, aggressive, and hardworking, while more mature boards are larger, less ego-involved, and more distant; both present challenges in being effectively managed.

13. *A board's behavior will often be a reflection of a recent crisis or radical change;* it is important that boards are not allowed to make decisions which are overshadowed by the "cumulative trauma" of historical problems that the organization or individual board members have experienced.

14. *No board is like any other;* each board, each board member must be managed to obtain the most from the relationship; likewise, each executive director must be adequately monitored and supported to get the most from the relationship.

15. *When these maxims are presented to a board and staff of an organization, both board and staff members will recognize the truth and value of most of the ideas, because of their experiences elsewhere, but they will question the applicability of these ideas to "this" organization;* interesting, isn't it?

This list should alert you to some of the aspects of board behavior of which you should be aware. Boards can be extremely useful, but they have to be managed. Board members never contribute automatically to an organization's functioning. Their contributions must be structured by the staff to come at the appropriate time and for the greatest impact. If your staff does not take the time to work with your board, you may find yourselves at odds over organizational policy, procedure or direction—a problem that could have been avoided.

BOARD RECRUITMENT

In order to ensure that your board is as useful as possible, there are a few guidelines for board recruitment that can be helpful.

First, your *board should be recruited with your annual plan in mind.* Once you have developed your program plan for the coming year and are clear about the longer-term directions of your organization, you will want to use these plans for guidance in determining the people who would be your best board members. Board recruitment is always easier and more effective when members can be approached to contribute to a specific plan already developed.

Second, a classic saying about volunteer board membership is that a *member's position should contribute wealth, work, or wisdom!* While many organizations have other criteria for board membership, this one constitutes a well-tested and workable guideline for specific contribution from individuals who accept the position. The specific mix you will be looking for will depend upon your plan and the needs of your organization as you see them over the coming year.

Third, in addition to providing a mixture of the three basic necessities of wealth, work, and wisdom, *your board members should represent various constituencies who are interested in your organization.* There should be representatives of the business community; the schools, if you call on them for facilities; local service clubs that may contribute money; and many other groups of direct or indirect relevance to the purposes of your group. The people you appoint should be as influential as possible, but they all should have a genuine interest in your organization.

Fourth, *you should recruit persons with specific expertise.* For example, it is always good to have someone from the local media who will know how to promote your activities. An attorney may be helpful on legal matters, and a leading businessperson or accountant can provide advice on financial matters. Men and women with professional backgrounds in these and other fields are obviously good material for your board. Again, the exact persons you will seek out will depend upon your program plan and your particular needs.

Fifth, *your need for fund-raising must always be kept in mind when you select some board members.* Well-known people will be most helpful in this aspect of your work. Their association with you provides not only visibility, but also credibility in the eyes of local people who may not be familiar with your work. In some cases, you may want to make your mayor or some other well-respected local person your honorary chairperson.

Finally, *your board members must be recruited with the knowledge that you want them and will personally seek their counsel and support their membership.* In the end, the desire to be needed and to work with a first-class staff member can be the two most important reasons that people agree to work on boards. While the cause is obviously of first importance, after that consideration board members choose the organization to work with based upon whether they feel their talents and skills are needed and on their desire to work with specific staff or other members of the board. It is imperative, therefore, that you consider your personal relationship with each board member and his or her compatibility with other members of the board in order to secure their maximum contribution.

Whatever the composition of your board and whatever its activities, it is important that the persons who serve on it share the same values and objectives as the officers and membership of your organization. When there is a sense of congruence and compatibility between the board members and staff of an organization, the maximum benefits will be gained by everyone and the organization will be most success-ful in its purpose.

MAKING YOUR "CORPORATE CULTURE" WORK FOR YOU

As a final section of this chapter on organization, it is important to acknowledge that groups operate not only according to formal structures, but also according to informal patterns, procedures, and relationships. This has been called by some people the "shadow" side of organizational life, because it represents how things *really* get done. One of the recent ways of describing the operating values and norms of organizations has been termed "corporate culture."[4] Let's see how this can apply to your local volunteer activities.

"Corporate culture" refers simply to *the way in which any group of people with shared goals and values work together over a period of time.* Given your work in international exchange, you know the importance of national culture in shaping the values and behavior of your foreign visitors and the people in your community. American organizational psychologists have suddenly discovered that organiza-tions, as well as countries, have "cultures." In other words, different organizations have different values and behavior that define the way in which people work together and how the organization relates to the rest of the world.

The two major building blocks of any organizational culture are *shared beliefs* and *norms of behavior.*

SHARED BELIEFS

We have already considered organizational beliefs in earlier chapters when we talked about "purpose." The beliefs of an organization are expressed in its mission statement and the way in which it allocates its resources to achieve its objectives. Organizations that believe in good communication and relationships between people will put a lot of time and energy into making sure that everyone understands what is going on and is fully participating in the direction of the organization. Other organizations that believe in servicing their customers or clients may place more resources against meeting the needs of the customer faster or better than anyone else. These are two different organizational beliefs that result in two different patterns of allocating resources.

NORMS OF BEHAVIOR

Norms of behavior are the expected, accepted, and supported ways in which people "do things around here." They are *expected* in that everyone knows that that's the way "things are done." They are *accepted,* because people believe in that way of working, or feel they can't change it. And the behavior is *supported,* because people actually feel this is the best way of behaving or acquiesce to others who "set the norms" in the organization.

It is important to realize that *norms may be positive or negative.* People in a local volunteer organization who believe it is important that everyone in their community should be aware of what they are doing may find various ways of spreading the word about their work. Every time foreign visitors come to the local Middletown Council for International Visitors, they are given a tour of the city, have a meeting with the mayor, and are interviewed by the local media. This is a norm for all visitors and a healthy contribution to the Middletown international visitors program in the community.

On the other hand, the same Middletown committee may have problems coordinating such activities, because their meetings never start on time and are poorly run. Since people expect that they never start on time and accept that as a norm, everyone feels at liberty to show up late. Since the president doesn't confront the issue and substitute the norm that meetings will start on time, regardless of whether everyone is there, meetings continue to start late and this pattern is supported by everyone who attends, even though everyone is bothered by it.

Likewise, when the Middletown meetings take place, the participants seem to have difficulty reaching conclusions, because there is a lack of agenda and focus in the way they are conducted. The president doesn't move the discussion along and it seems very hard to come to a clear decision regarding who will have responsibility to get things done in what kind of time frame. As a result, while local publicity is obtained, it is done mostly by the publicity coordinator acting on her own; the meetings never produce the kind of coordination they are supposed to. Since neither the publicity coordinator nor anyone else stops and says "Let's look at how we are working together and try to change our norms," the negative norms continue to be expected, accepted, and supported by people's lack of willingness, capacity, or skills to change.

It is important that every organization be aware not only of roles and responsibilities set out in job descriptions, but how these roles and responsibilities are carried out by the people who hold them. In many instances people may not do their job well, not because they lack the skills, but because the norms of the group dictate negative ways of working together.

MANAGING YOUR ORGANIZATIONAL CULTURE

To manage your group's culture, there are two easy steps you need to take: first, recognize your positive and negative norms; second, be willing to talk about them with one another in a way which allows you to change them.

To recognize your positive and negative norms you might use a questionnaire like the one in Figure 3.[5] This checklist of twenty characteristics of "healthy" and "unhealthy" organizations admittedly carries a bias in terms of organizational norms, but it will give you one way to test your group's way of doing things. If you disagree with the implicit philosophy or values in this questionnaire, your group can do its own exercise to identify your norms. Have everyone write down on a sheet of paper the "Things we do around here that are helpful to our work together" and the "Things we do around here that hurt the way we work together." Then list these on a blackboard or flipchart and use them as the basis for making everyone aware of your group's "culture."

Figure 3

Twenty Characteristics of Unhealthy and Healthy Volunteer Chapters

---

A Checklist

I. Mission and Purpose

Unhealthy

1.   There is little personal investment in our chapter's objectives except by the officers.

Frequently _____ Sometimes _____ Never _____

Healthy

1.   Our chapter's objectives are widely shared by our members, and there is a strong and consistent flow of energy toward those objectives.

Frequently _____ Sometimes _____ Never _____

Unhealthy

2.   Tradition is important in determining program activities and ways of doing things.

Frequently _____ Sometimes _____ Never _____

Healthy

2.   Innovation and new ideas are encouraged within the context of the chapter's overall mission and purpose.

Frequently _____ Sometimes _____ Never _____

Unhealthy

3.   Our programs are perfunctory and lifeless, inspiring little enthusiasm. People attend because of habit or obligation.

Frequently _____ Sometimes _____ Never _____

Healthy

3.   Our programs are stimulating, providing enjoyment and a service to the people who participate in them.

Frequently _____ Sometimes _____ Never _____

Figure 3 Continued

Twenty Characteristics of Unhealthy and Healthy Volunteer Chapters

---

A Checklist

II. Structure

Unhealthy

4. Our chapter is comprised of an "in group" which resists persons joining from other parts of the community.

   Frequently _____ Sometimes _____ Never _____

Healthy

4. There is an active membership recruitment program to bring new blood into our chapter.

   Frequently _____ Sometimes _____ Never _____

Unhealthy

5. People feel locked into their stale responsibilities, bored and constrained by the fact that there is no one else to do the work.

   Frequently _____ Sometimes _____ Never _____

Healthy

5. People are involved in and committed to their responsibilities from which they receive a great deal of satisfaction.

   Frequently _____ Sometimes _____ Never _____

Unhealthy

6. Our chapter's structure, policies, and procedures encumber people.

   Frequently _____ Sometimes _____ Never _____

Healthy

6. Our chapter's structure, procedures, and policies are fashioned to help people get the job done and to protect the long-term health of the organization.

   Frequently _____ Sometimes _____ Never _____

Figure 3 Continued

Twenty Characteristics of Unhealthy and Healthy Volunteer Chapters

A Checklist

III. Leadership and Communications

Unhealthy

7. Communication is poor and creates many problems.

Frequently _____ Sometimes _____ Never _____

Healthy

7. People easily get the information they need to do their jobs.

Frequently _____ Sometimes _____ Never _____

Unhealthy

8. Relationships are contaminated by "gamesmanship." People lack concern for one another and are not able to be themselves.

Frequently _____ Sometimes _____ Never _____

Healthy

8. Relationships are open. People care about one another and are able to be themselves.

Frequently _____ Sometimes _____ Never _____

IV. Teamwork

Unhealthy

9. People in our chapter see things going wrong, but do nothing about it. Mistakes and problems are habitually ignored or shelved.

Frequently _____ Sometimes _____ Never _____.

Healthy

9. People feel free to discuss their feelings about difficulties, because they are optimistic that the chapter members have the willingness and ability to deal with them constructively.

Frequently _____ Sometimes _____ Never _____

Figure 3 Continued

Twenty Characteristics of Unhealthy and Healthy Volunteer Chapters

A Checklist

Unhealthy

10. A few people try to control as many decisions as possible. They often make decisions based upon inadequate information or consultation.

    Frequently _____ Sometimes _____ Never _____

Healthy

10. Many people share in decision-making, depending upon such factors as ability, responsibility, and availability

    Frequently _____ Sometimes _____ Never _____

Unhealthy

11. A few people feel they are alone in trying to get things done.

    Frequently _____ Sometimes _____ Never _____

Healthy

11. There is a noticeable sense of teamwork in planning and a sharing of responsibility in getting things done.

    Frequently _____ Sometimes _____ Never _____

Unhealthy

12. People compete when they need to collaborate. They are very jealous of their area of responsibility. Seeking or accepting help is felt to be a sign of weakness.

    Frequently _____ Sometimes _____ Never _____

Healthy

12. Collaboration is encouraged. People readily request help and are willing to give in return.

    Frequently _____ Sometimes _____ Never _____

Figure 3 Continued

Twenty Characteristics of Unhealthy and Healthy Volunteer Chapters

A Checklist

Unhealthy

13.   People swallow their frustrations: "I can't do anything. It's *their* responsibility to save this project, not mine."

Frequently _____ Sometimes _____ Never _____

Healthy

13.   Frustrations bring people to talk to one another. "It's my/our responsibility to save this project; let's see what the problem is."

Frequently _____ Sometimes _____ Never _____

Unhealthy

14.   Conflicts are mostly covert, managed by politics and other games. There are some long-standing issues which are never confronted and that continue to plague interpersonal relations and chapter effectiveness.

Frequently _____ Sometimes _____ Never _____

Healthy

14.   Conflicts are considered important to decision-making and personal growth. They are dealt with effectively and openly.

Frequently _____ Sometimes _____ Never _____

Unhealthy

15.   When there is a crisis, people withdraw or start blaming one another.

Frequently _____ Sometimes _____ Never _____

Healthy

15.   When there is a crisis, people quickly band together and work until the crisis is over.

Frequently _____ Sometimes _____ Never _____

Figure 3 Continued

Twenty Characteristics of Unhealthy and Healthy Volunteer Chapters

---

A Checklist

V. Resource Management

Unhealthy

16. Fund-raising is seen as a responsibility which one or two people grudgingly take on because they've been badgered into it.

Frequently _____ Sometimes _____ Never _____

Healthy

16. Everyone joins in fund-raising projects and thinks of ways of making them fun.

Frequently _____ Sometimes _____ Never _____

Unhealthy

17. Our chapter's mission and goals are unknown and therefore likely not to attract members of the community to support us.

Frequently _____ Sometimes _____ Never _____

Healthy

17. Our chapter is known and respected in the community as a worthwhile cause.

Frequently _____ Sometimes _____ Never _____

Unhealthy

18. Poor performance is glossed over or dealt with indirectly.

Frequently _____ Sometimes _____ Never _____

Healthy

18. Poor performance is discussed with those involved. People seek and offer help so as to do better next time.

Frequently _____ Sometimes _____ Never _____

Figure 3 Continued

Twenty Characteristics of Unhealthy and Healthy Volunteer Chapters

---

A Checklist

Unhealthy

19. Review of personal and chapter success and failure is avoided.

Frequently _____ Sometimes _____ Never _____

Healthy

19. Joint critique of chapter's failure and success is routine within each planning cycle.

Frequently _____ Sometimes _____ Never _____

Unhealthy

20. Our club is mostly work!

Frequently _____ Sometimes _____ Never _____

Healthy

20. Our club is fun!

Frequently _____ Sometimes _____ Never _____

Obviously, it is one thing to recognize and acknowledge your group's culture, it is another to change it. To determine changes you want to make you should look at *both* the positive and the negative list. The reason for this is to ensure that in changing something negative, you don't lose something that is positive and more highly valued.

For example, as a way of controlling meetings, you might decide that you will not allow any discussion of items not on an agenda in advance of a meeting. You might also find, however, that one of your positive norms that has been very helpful for your group has been spontaneous discussions, which many times have led to unforeseen creative ideas and projects that have been highly successful.

In other words, you need to look at all aspects of your culture and change only those areas that will result in a more positive *overall* experience.

When considering a discussion like this, it might also be useful to return to Chapter 1, in which I discuss some of the useful ways of relating to people that Carl Rogers has outlined. These are also norms of behavior, based upon a value of openness and honesty in communication. If you share these, you might use them as the basis of your group's review of your culture. Certainly Rogers's caveats regarding "listening openly and acceptantly to yourself and others" would be high on the list of applicable behavior during this kind of meeting.

So there you have it. "Corporate culture" unraveled. It's not so difficult. In some ways it is amazing that American corporations are finding it such a fascination as a result of the recent book, *In Search of Excellence* by Thomas Peters and Robert Waterman. If you are interested in exploring the issue further, I highly recommend the book. It is very readable and will be an extremely important contribution to U.S. management thinking for many years to come.

For Further Study

Allen, Robert F. and Charlotte Craft. *Beat the System! A Way to Create More Humane Environments.* New York: McGraw-Hill, 1980.

_____. *The Organizational Unconscious: How to Create the Corporate Culture You Want and Need.* Englewood Cliffs, N.J.: Prentice-Hall, 1982.

Conrad, William and William Glenn. *The Effective Voluntary Board of Directors: What It Is and How It Works.* Chicago: The Swallow Press, Inc., 1980, 3rd ed.

Drucker, Peter F. *Management: Tasks, Responsibilities, Practices.* New York: Harper & Row, 1974.

Fordyce, Jack K. and Raymond Weil. *Managing with People: A Manager's Handbook of Organization Development Methods.* Reading, Mass.: Addison-Wesley, 1971.

Mathiasen III, Karl. "The Board of Directors of Nonprofit Organizations." Washington, D.C.: Center for Community Change, 1977.

Peters, Thomas J. and Robert H. Waterman, Jr. *In Search of Excellence: Lessons from America's Best-Run Companies.* New York: Harper & Row, 1982.

Wilson, Marlene. *The Effective Management of Volunteer Programs.* Boulder, Colorado: Volunteer Management Associates, 1976, Chapters 4 and 6.

Part II:

MANAGING YOUR RESOURCES: PEOPLE, PROGRAMS AND FINANCES

Recruiting and Motivating Volunteers

5

As the leader of a volunteer effort, your ultimate success rests with the people you attract to work with you and the way in which you lead and motivate them to contribute their time and energy to your organization.

The leadership and management of volunteers has changed dramatically over the last twenty years as dual-career marriages, the women's movement, and greater concern for self-development have changed traditional attitudes of women volunteers. Before turning to a review of techniques for recruiting and motivating volunteers, therefore, let us attempt to understand better some of the changes that have taken place in the U.S. volunteer population in recent years.

THE CHANGING CONTEXT OF VOLUNTEERISM TODAY

A Gallup survey on volunteering in the Fall of 1983 revealed that 92 million Americans—55 percent of the adult population—volunteered in 1982.[1] But there were major new trends in the characteristics of these volunteers:

1. While traditionally, the bulk of volunteers have been married women who did not work outside the home, today more than two-thirds of the women between twenty-five and forty-four are employed. Furthermore, 57 percent of married women

with children work outside the home. So *there are far fewer traditional volunteers available.*

2.   As a result working people are now the fastest-growing segment of the volunteer work force. Forty-one percent of the volunteers are male and many more retired persons and youth are volunteering. Consequently, *volunteers today are more frequently:*

professional men and women with extremely busy, complex personal lives

young people with little tolerance for poor organization of activities, or

older retired persons, many of whom have held important responsibilities during their lives.

As a result, *they are less willing to tolerate poorly managed programs, regardless of how "good" the intentions of ineffective volunteer leaders might be.*

3.   The need for volunteers has increased dramatically over the last twenty years as new causes have been initiated and new issues and needs have entered society's consciousness. The *competition for volunteer time* has placed additional pressure on ensuring that more "traditional" areas of volunteerism, such as international exchange, can develop new, innovative ways to encourage continued support of movements in the face of other priorities and needs on a national and international level.

All of this adds up to a mandate for more effective management of our volunteer organizations if we are to continue to attract the kind of people we want for our international exchange activities. The implications of the trends reported in the Gallup Poll dictate the following conclusions:

More attention should be paid to retired persons, many of whom have traditionally not seen themselves as volunteers for international exchange programs. There is tremendous opportunity to call on the international experience of older people in working with international visitors to your community. But it will be necessary to develop a campaign aimed specifically at the older volunteer.

New strategies must be developed to involve as many junior high and high school students as possible in international exchange activities. While young people have traditionally been a source of support in many communities involved in youth exchanges, other organizations will be increasingly recruiting them for their own causes as a result of the lessened availability of the traditional nonworking women volunteers. International exchange organizations must therefore pay particular attention to the young people they have relied on in the past to ensure that they are not lost to other activities.

New strategies must be sought for attracting and retaining working people—both men and women. Local activities and events, meeting times and responsibilities must be re-examined and geared to busy people with limited available time. The fact that people are working is no excuse for their not becoming involved in volunteer activities. The challenge to volunteer organizations today is to ensure that busy people will feel satisfied and rewarded as a result of contributing their limited free time to your effort.

Finally, our volunteer organizations must be better managed and led to ensure that the programs are of high quality, are effectively planned, organized, and implemented, and are utilizing the precious limited resources of money and volunteer time as wisely as possible. To do this will in many cases take a new awareness and new actions by many volunteer leaders.

In the following discussion of volunteer recruitment, motivation, and leadership, we shall keep in mind the profile of these "new" volunteers as we examine ways to attract and keep their commitment to international exchanges.

KEYS TO RECRUITMENT: IDEALISM, RISK–TAKING, AND REWARDS

There are *three keys* to recruiting volunteers. We must *call on their altruism and idealism, deal with their fears,* and *demonstrate the personal rewards and understanding that they can gain* from the experience.

IDEALISM

We have already discussed the altruistic aspects of international exchanges in Chapter 2. International peace and understanding and the transfer of knowledge and technology for greater world development are the two major factors usually emphasized.

Unfortunately, we too often proudly articulate the idealistic virtues of our programs without paying attention to two pragmatic, personal questions that volunteers ask: "What will I risk?" and "What will I gain?"

We must be prepared to point to our own local organization and the volunteer opportunities available in terms of the way in which these can provide a chance for people to learn and grow. At the same time we must help them overcome initial fears and hesitations they may have about international activities. Let's look further into these two challenges.

RISK–TAKING

In starting to recruit volunteers for international exchange programs, we are faced with two psychological challenges. The first we have already noted: A potential volunteer may have had no close international association or experience to predispose him or her to work for international exchange.

But there is a second, equally difficult barrier to overcome—the fear of the unknown. The fact is that volunteering for a cross-cultural experience means *taking a risk*. People who are involved in community hosting programs take the risk of opening their homes, their family, and themselves to someone from another culture, someone with different values, different beliefs, and different style of living. They take the risk of feeling uncomfortable with cross-cultural differences, of having difficulty communicating, and of embarrassment when misunderstandings arise. Then there are always the few international visitors who are problem personalities. Let's face it—many people shy away from an international hosting program because they are afraid that they may be saddled with a social misfit.

Likewise, for those who decide to go abroad for home hospitality, the risks are the same in reverse. The risk of being in a foreign society where you may not speak the language. The risk of being dependent upon a family you have never met before. The risk of embarrassment as you learn cultural differences and values the hard way. The risk of learning something about yourself that you did not want to know.

The fear of taking a risk is often a much greater barrier to recruiting volunteers for international exchange programs than is the lack of time. To counter that fear, there is, of course, the old adage "Nothing ventured, nothing gained." And it is certainly true of experiences in human relations, both in this country and abroad.

If we can find ways to help people overcome their fear of committing themselves to an experience with someone they have never met, the basic psychological resistance to hosting programs whose goal is international understanding through people-to-people relations will be overcome.

Based on experience and the psychological literature, it appears that *the best way to approach people about the potential risks involved in international exchange is to talk about them.* One of the biggest mistakes many of us make is to avoid acknowledging what other people are feeling and dealing with it. We are afraid that if we raise the issue we will scare people off. The fact is that people are being scared off anyway, because *they* recognize and feel the risks. If we don't find a way to help them deal with this discomfort and overcome it, all of our other arguments for volunteering will be useless.

One of the most challenging volunteer recruitment situations faced by many youth exchange organizations today is finding families willing to host a foreign student for a year. If you are in this situation, you might want to follow the following guidelines in talking with prospective host families:

Be specific about the risks. Usually, they involve:

Fear of not being able to communicate across language differences

Fear of "problem personalities" or a lack of "fit" between people hosted and their family

Fear of not being able to get out of a bad experience

Fear of not having enough time to play host properly and develop interesting things to do

Fear of the costs involved

Fear of the unknown and a new experience, either in one's own community or abroad

For each risk, talk about your own experience and feelings when you first thought about becoming involved in international exchanges. Tell them how you overcame your concerns and how, when your worst fears may have come true (possibly you had a "problem personality" to deal with), you handled the situation successfully.

For each risk, outline the policies and procedures your organization uses to deal with it and demonstrate how you are prepared to help when difficulties arise.

In the end, stress the fact that *every gain in personal development always involves some risk;* that developing international friendships and new international perspectives, like everything in life that has rewards, has some risks; that ultimately volunteering for international exchange is worth it and that *they should try it on a limited basis, with your personal support and interest,* until they feel comfortable with it and want to commit to it for a longer time.

If you can make this kind of personal commitment in recruiting and working with volunteers of all kinds, you will have taken a first important step in attracting and motivating them to work for your organization.

PERSONAL REWARDS

For years, programs in international exchange have appealed to people to "take a foreign visitor into your home" or "contribute your time to better world understanding."

While a commitment to an ideal-like world understanding or a better relationship among peoples of the world may be one underlying motivation for people to become involved in international exchange programs, we must remember that *people are increasingly motivated to participate in those activities that best meet their short-term needs and long-term objectives.*

This is not selfish—it is natural. Historically, there has been an unfortunate tendency for volunteers to downgrade the fact that volunteer projects should produce volunteer satisfaction as well as community service. The old Protestant ethic of self-sacrifice has traditionally been so well incorporated into most volunteer organizations that unless people believed they were working totally for others they felt they were somehow performing less than the ideal community service.

This is no longer primarily the case, as we have discussed earlier. Volunteers today are increasingly identifying their own needs to be met. More women are working than ever before. There is a higher likelihood than ever that a volunteer will also hold a full-time job. Thus volunteers have less time and more experience in working in personally fulfilling organizational roles. As a result, they approach volunteer work with a much more critical perspective than ever before, both because they have less time and also more experience in organizational life.

To put it very simply, volunteers today demand better management and leadership and refuse to allow for the "good intentions" with which many unprepared volunteer leaders have led programs in the past. So all organizations are being increasingly pressed to find volunteer leaders able to meet new standards of leadership more akin to those of management in the business world. This is a difficult challenge, but one that is being increasingly recognized by all volunteer organizations and responded to with new training programs and manuals to help local volunteers develop management and leadership knowledge and skills. This guide is one such response to the challenge.

In recruiting volunteers, then, you should begin with a statement concerning the purpose of your organization and its role in your community, but do not forget to deal with the way in which your group can provide important, fulfilling opportunities for prospective volunteers that will meet the needs they may have in their own lives.

MOTIVATION: MEETING NEEDS

To be more attuned to helping volunteers meet their needs, it is important to understand some of the basic needs that people meet through volunteering. Let's see what some of the popular psychological theories tell us about volunteer motivation.

The first thing to understand about motivation is that *to motivate somebody one must do something that holds the promise of meeting his or her needs.* While people have a range of physical needs—shelter, security, food, sleep—they also have a range of social needs, including the need to be with others, the need for recognition, and the need for self-development and improvement.

One well-known psychologist who has contributed a great deal to theories about volunteer motivation is David C. McClelland, whose work on motivation led him to the description of "achievement motivation" as a key driving force behind American economic prosperity.[2] McClelland's work revealed that there are three basic needs met by social interaction, and are therefore important to organizational life, whether at work or in volunteer organizations. These were: the need for affiliation, for power, and for achievement.

NEED FOR AFFILIATION

Many volunteers have a strong need for affiliation. A *need for affiliation is indicated when a person enjoys being with people and establishing friendships.* It is *not* implicit in wanting to do something for another person. I will explain this difference more fully in a moment.

A person with a high need for affiliation

- Would rather be with others than alone

- Is more concerned about the interpersonal aspects of his or her volunteer work than with the work itself

- Seeks the approval of others, and

- Performs volunteer tasks more effectively when working with others in a cooperative atmosphere than when working alone or in a high conflict situation

The social aspect of volunteer work attracts people who have a high need for affiliation. Most volunteer activities take place in groups, which provide a sense of satisfaction for affiliation-motivated persons. Many volunteer activities, like international exchange, are dedicated to well-respected causes. By volunteering, affiliation-motivated people gain the approval of others for providing a useful community service.

Volunteer service can therefore be highly satisfying to a person with this motivation.

We shall see in a moment how these people can be best utilized in volunteer work.

NEED FOR POWER

Many volunteers are motivated by a need for power, although few recognize it and those who do tend to be embarrassed about it. This is, of course, ridiculous, because if organizations did not have some people with a need for power, there would be little leadership.

Essentially, *an individual with a need for power wants to have an impact on others.* This kind of person

- Is sensitive to the interpersonal influences in any group or organization

- Is active in the politics of any organization of which he or she is a member

- Joins organizations that are prestigious, and sometimes

- Attempts to help others without being requested to do so

People who become involved in the leadership and determination of policy for organizations, including volunteer organizations, should do so because they enjoy it; that is, *they should need to have an impact on other people.* In most organizations, this need can be fulfilled constructively through leading or representing the organization on behalf of its members. This social motivation becomes counterproductive only when the individual's needs for prestige and recognition are placed ahead of the need to represent the collective interests of all the organization's members. This has been characterized as the difference between the need for *social power (on behalf of the collective interests of an organization) and personal power (solely on behalf of one's own image, status, and position).*

People with a high need for power, however, may be attracted to volunteer organizations for a less productive reason. Researchers have found that *one of the negative characteristics of people with a high need for power is that they occasionally attempt to help others without being requested to do so.* Many people who see themselves as providing much-needed assistance to others through counseling or social work are in fact sometimes meeting their own need to have an impact on others more than they are meeting people's real needs to be helped. This desire to "rush in and fix things," which I referred to in Chapter 1, must be controlled for successful service work.

NEED FOR ACHIEVEMENT

All volunteer groups contain people who have a high need for achievement. *A need for achievement is indicated when someone wants to perform better than he or she ever has before.* A person with this motivation

- Prefers situations in which success depends more on personal talents and skills than on chance

- Seeks out situations in which the risk is moderate and proportionate to his or her resources for coping with it

- Needs concrete feedback on performance and knowledge of results he or she has achieved, and

- Tends to think ahead in anticipation of future possibilities

Obviously, the "achiever" is an independent, self-directed person who can take responsibility for a task and get it done. America has been called the achieving society, and in many ways achievement behavior is classic American behavior. This is true not only of the for-profit world, but also of the not-for-profit world.

Over the years people have tended to believe that those who have a strong need to achieve are concerned only about money and financial gain. In fact, research has shown that this just isn't true. People who are successful businesspersons are often driven not by a need to accumulate great amounts of wealth, but by a need to take a moderate risk and receive feedback on their performance. The feedback is the profit margin!

In not-for-profit or voluntary organizations, there is obviously no profit margin. There is a "satisfaction margin," however, and it is important that we provide opportunities for volunteers to get satisfaction (feedback) from their activities. One responsibility of being a volunteer leader, therefore, is to structure situations in which people can feel successful when they have achieved their goals. This is one of the reasons why we stressed goals so strongly in our earlier discussion of organizational planning. Ultimately, organizational achievement rests upon personal achievement. Thus, it is important to recruit and include within your membership people who have a high need for achievement.

MATCHING NEEDS AND VOLUNTEER ROLES

We have taken time to review McClelland's theories not only because they are relevant to volunteer motivation, but also to emphasize that one of the ways you "motivate" volunteers is by being sensitive to their needs and how your organization can meet these needs.

This leads to two points which must be emphasized about the three social motivations just described:

Almost everyone has each of the three needs—affiliation, power and achievement—in some degree.

Psychologists have discovered, however, that at different times in people's lives and with different personalities, these needs will vary in strength. We can therefore speak of some people who are more highly motivated by a need for affiliation than by a need for power or achievement and other people who are motivated by a need for both achievement and power, but have little need for affiliation.

Every successful organization utilizes a range of people with varying motivational patterns.

Good managers recognize that different roles require people with different motivations. These leaders are sensitive to the needs of their members and attempt to place them in organizational roles that will meet their needs as well as the needs of the organization.

This is one of the reasons we noted in Chapter 1 that "good leadership starts with caring about people." Different roles demand different personalities and styles. For example, organization presidents should be people who have a high need for achievement and power, since they will be responsible for directing activities, setting goals, receiving feedback, evaluating performance, searching for creative ideas, and persuading members and others to support the group's objectives.

People who work on home hospitality projects will probably be people who have a higher need for affiliation than for power. These are people who enjoy being with others, like the interpersonal aspect of their volunteer work, and seek out new people to whom they can relate in a warm and friendly atmosphere.

On the other hand, a person whose greatest felt need is for power will probably make a good publicity chairperson. In this position, his or her prime concern with influencing others on behalf of the organization will stand in good stead.

Think of the times you have not really enjoyed an assignment you were given. It was probably because you were in a job in which you didn't feel comfortable. Another way of describing it is to say that the job didn't meet your needs. It is important in your work with volunteers to help them examine what needs they want to meet through their work in your organization.

LEADERSHIP AND MOTIVATION

A third important aspect of motivating volunteers, in addition to recognizing their needs and giving them responsibilities that meet these needs, is proper leadership style. The "one-man show" is a debilitating problem of many small volunteer organizations.

Oddly enough, experience has proven that strong, forceful, dynamic leaders who take on massive responsibilities for themselves many times mean the death knell for their organizations. There are two reasons for this.

First, a leader who does not delegate sufficiently fails to challenge others around him. As a result, the best people will go to other organizations where they can take on responsibility and feel a sense of accomplishment.

Second, a leader who works day and night handling all the major functions of a group is not training other people to take over when the time comes to step down. As a result, when that person retires or moves away, the local volunteer group may fall apart, because no other leadership has been developed.

A final aspect of the overly strong leader is that he sets a role model for the leadership position, which is not only disfunctional, but unrealistic for most other people. As a result, there is not only a lack of training, but also a great reluctance by other people to take on the responsibility, because most could never give the time and energy to the job that the original dedicated leader did.

Problems of delegation and strong leadership are only part of the story, however. Recent research on leadership has revealed that strong, directive leadership is only one of several styles that can be used to meet different organizational and individual needs.[3] Other appropriate ones are "consultative," in which you suggest a direction, but ask other people's reaction before making a decision, and "participative," in which you identify a problem and ask everyone in the group to help in finding a solution. Of course, the best leadership style is often to delegate responsibility completely to someone whom you know can handle the task alone!

FEEDBACK AND MOTIVATION

By now it should be clear that one of the most critical actions necessary for motivating volunteers is to allow them to receive feedback on their performance. Achievement-motivated people thrive on feedback about the accomplishment of their goals; affiliation-motivated people seek feedback that they are liked; and power-motivated people want to know if you are impressed by their actions. *Everyone* needs feedback.

But guess what? Feedback seems to be the hardest thing to find, especially in volunteer organizations where people are afraid of hurting one another's feelings. Positive feedback comes more easily (although not more often) than corrective feedback. Corrective or negative feedback tends to come anonymously, because people in volunteer organizations are normally very hesitant to confront one another with concerns about behavior and performance.

If you are going to have a healthy organization and healthy relationships with the people with whom you work, however, you are going to have to establish a norm of clear, specific, and timely feedback. Figure 4 lists a series of characteristics of feedback that people have found important over the years. I would suggest you look them over and think them through. There are many valuable insights and lessons in this short list.

In addition to this general list of things to keep in mind, Figure 5 provides a "script" you can use.

This may seem like a great deal of detail, but I believe that providing negative feedback and confronting conflict is such a vital area for a healthy organization (and is so dreadfully underdeveloped in volunteer organizations) that it is important for you to have as many tools as possible in working with your people on this area. Remember, *all* the research and theories say that *people need feedback!*

A final source you may want to consult in thinking about your leadership style and its relationship to the motivation of your volunteers is the recent book by Kenneth Blanchard and Spencer Johnson entitled *The One Minute Manager.*[4] The message of this small volume is simple. There are three things necessary for managing effective performance. These are:

- one-minute goal-settings

- one-minute praisings

- one-minute reprimands

The assumption is that if all of your volunteers have goals that they can check in one minute to see how they are doing against their target, they will be more motivated and better able to manage their own performance. Furthermore, if you can take one minute to praise or correct behavior that you see as particularly right or wrong *when it happens,* you will have a much greater impact on performance than if you store up all your reactions and feelings and let them all come out in some unconstructive or less meaningful way.

This certainly fits with the characteristics of effective feedback with achievement motivation and with the planning process we discussed in Chapter 3. You will find as we continue throughout this volume that these fundamentals of mission, goals and feedback will be relevant for many different aspects of management.

Figure 4

Characteristics of Helpful Feedback

The giving and receiving of feedback is a skill that can be acquired. When feedback is attempted at the wrong time or given in the wrong way the results will be at best useless, and may be disastrous. Therefore, developing feedback skills can be important. Here are some criteria for useful feedback:

It is descriptive rather than evaluative. It is helpful to focus on what the individual *did* rather than to translate his behavior into a statement about what he *is*. "You have interrupted three people in the last half hour" is probably not something that a person really wants to hear, but it is likely to be more helpful than "You are a bad-mannered oaf."

It focuses on the feelings generated in the person who has experienced the behavior and who is offering the feedback. "When you interrupt me I feel frustrated," gives the individual clear information about the *effect* of his behavior, while at the same time leaving him free to decide what he wants to do about that effect.

It is specific rather than general. For example, it is probably more useful to learn that you "talk too much" than to have someone describe you as "dominating."

It is solicited rather than imposed. Feedback is most useful when the receiver feels that he needs and wants it, when he himself has formulated the kind of question which those observing him can answer.

It is well-timed. In general, feedback is most useful at the earliest opportunity after the given behavior depending, of course, on the receiver's readiness to hear it, on the support available from others, and so on.

It is not given to "dump" or "unload" on another. If you feel you *have* to say this to the other person, then ask yourself who it is you are trying to "help."

Feedback does not ask "Why?" It stays within the bounds of behavior and one's reactions to that behavior. To theorize about or ask why a person does a certain thing is to plumb the depths of motivation and, perhaps, of the unconscious. Avoiding the "whys" will help one to avoid the error of amateur psychologizing.

Figure 5

Confronting a Volunteer Productively**

When you have a problem with a volunteer, you should follow the following ten-step procedure for arriving at a productive solution.

Step 1. *Set a time and place to talk.* "I want to discuss with you an issue that concerns both of us. When and where would be a good place to do this?" (Agree on a time and place. Be sure to provide enough time and insure complete privacy.)

Step 2. (When you have arrived at the appropriate spot), *State your intentions and expectations for the outcome of this meeting.* "I intend to raise an issue about a certain way we are working together. I hope we can join together to create a solution that will be agreeable to you as well as me."

Step 3. *State the event.* "Remember when . . . " (Wait for acknowledgment.)

Step 4. *State your feelings about the event and end your statement with a question.* "When you . . . I felt . . . I felt that way because I wanted . . . How were you feeling?

Step 5. *Explore all relevant information concerning the event.* "I'd like to tell you my view of what happened and I want to hear your side also." DO NOT GO FOR SOLUTIONS YET.

Step 6. *Repeat the volunteer's view of the event.* "OK, let me see if I understand your statements. What you're saying is . . . "

Step 7. *Explore solutions that would satisfy both of you.* "Maybe now that I understand what you were thinking about and you understand what I was thinking about, we can explore some ways to solve this kind of thing in the future."
1. What can I do to make you more effective?
2. Here's what you can do to make me more effective.

Step 8. *Offer a fair exchange.* "OK, I'll perform this for you in the future, if you perform what I want you to do in exchange."

Step 9. *Test for agreement and commitment.* "Do you really think we can carry this bargain out? What will we do if someone breaks their half of the agreement?"

Step 10. *Sum up.* I think we have agreed that . . .

**Reproduced from *Managing Volunteers for Results* by Audrey Richards, Institute for Fund Raising, 333 Hayes Street, San Francisco, Calif. 94102; 1978.

A RECRUITING STRATEGY FOR VOLUNTEERS

Finally, we come to recruitment. It should be obvious by now that the most effective recruiting strategy is developed when you can (1) articulate the idealistic purposes of your organization, (2) outline the plans and goals you have for the coming year, (3) explain your group's structure and the jobs which need to be filled, and (4) describe the personal needs a potential volunteer might meet by working with you.

Armed with this kind of information, you are prepared to mount a membership-recruitment campaign which should strengthen and enhance your volunteer group. Figure 6 contains a list of where you might go to find potential volunteers. Here are a few guidelines to keep in mind about volunteer recruitment.[5]

1. Do specific, rather than general, recruiting whenever possible.

    Choose appropriate audiences whose interests and priorities match your needs.

    Determine who has the skills you need and actively seek them out; you can find new members among all the constituencies you serve. The list in Figure 6 includes a range of people who might be tapped by your group. You can probably add other targets to your list. Don't try to go after too many groups at once; instead, plan a concentrated campaign among the people whom you feel would be most interested in your activities.

    Be as specific and honest in your appeal as possible about the time and commitment it will take.

2. Have a year-round recruitment plan.

3. Utilize a variety of recruitment techniques.

    Newspapers, radio/TV, posters, billboards, bumper stickers, presentations and speeches, brochures, displays, person-to-person, tours and open houses, newsletters.

Figure 6

TARGET POPULATIONS
Where Are the Volunteers?

COMMUNITY GROUPS

Chambers of Commerce
Jaycees
Churches
Local Nonprofit Foundations
Rotary Clubs
Lions Clubs
Kiwanis Clubs
PTA
Women's Clubs
Garden Clubs
United Funds
YMCAs, YWCAs
HI–YIs
Associations

Teen Canteens
Boy Scouts
Girl Scouts

Historical Societies
Intercultural Associations
Hobby Clubs
Fraternal Organizations
Youth Clubs
Ethnic Organizations
American Legion
Other Veterans Organizations
4-H Clubs
School Associations
Sports Associations
Professional Associations
Retired Senior Volunteer Program, American Association of Retired Persons
Special Interest Groups
Social Welfare Organizations
Other _____

INDIVIDUAL PROSPECTS

Major Givers
Supporters of Your Organization Club
Friends and Relatives
High School Students
Retired Persons
Parents of School-aged Children
Program Alumni
Tourists

Clients (Buyers of a Service)
School International Relations

Teachers
Grammar School Children
Professional People
Employees of Local Companies
Local Government Officials
Other _____

BUSINESSES

National Businesses
Local Businesses
Banks
Local Retailers
Shopping Center Associations
Unions
Businessmen's Associations

Trade Groups
Office Building Tenants
Corporate Executives
Wholesalers
The Media
Entertainment Businesses
Other _____

4. Recruit by inviting people to respond to the opportunity to volunteer, not by telling them they *ought* to be concerned and involved in your cause.

5. Be enthusiastic!

6. Expand opportunities to volunteer to all segments of your community.

Recruiting, motivating, and leading volunteers is the central responsibility in managing your organization. If you can successfully apply the principles outlined in this chapter, all of the program management, which we will discuss in the next part of this book, can be carried out by other people!

For Further Study

Blanchard, Kenneth and Spencer Johnson. *The One Minute Manager.* New York: William Morrow and Company, 1982.

Cribbin, James J. *Effective Managerial Leadership.* New York: American Management Association, 1972.

_____. *Leadership: Strategies for Organizational Effectiveness.* New York: American Management Association, 1981.

Hersey, Paul and Kenneth H. Blanchard. *Management of Organizational Behavior: Utilizing Human Resources.* 3rd ed., Englewood Cliffs, N.J.: Prentice-Hall, 1977.

"How to Get a Man," *Voluntary Action Leadership.* Fall 1975. National Center for Voluntary Action, 1214 16th St., N.W., Washington, D.C., 20036.

McClelland, David C. *The Achieving Society.* Princeton, N.J.: Van Nostrand, 1961.

Naylor, Harriet H. *Volunteers Today: Finding, Training and Working with Them.* New York: Dryden, 1973.

Pell, Arthur A. *Recruitment, Training and Motivating Volunteer Workers.* New York: Pilot Books, 1972.

Gaining Support Through Publicity

6

While people may be your most important resource in a volunteer organization, a clear public image is critical for their recruitment. Publicity is the lifeblood of every organization's existence. You don't *have* to have publicity, but unless you do, your group may be traveling on a one-way street to oblivion!

This chapter contains ideas and techniques that can be undertaken by almost anyone. It is best, however, that the responsibility for publicity be given to a specific person designated as your publicity coordinator. This should preferably be someone who is interested and can take the time to cultivate the contacts necessary to make your organization known in the community.

Most publicity functions can be handled from your own home—a telephone and typewriter are the essential tools. However, there should be some visits to newspapers and radio/television studios (those applicable to your local situation), and you will probably also want to make some friends in a local print shop. The publicity coordinator should, of course, play an active role in your group, attending meetings and all special events. If she takes an active interest in the development of events, she will find it easier to communicate with the public about them.

The chief requirement for the person in charge of publicity is, in fact, an interest in the work. With the right attitude, the job can be one of the most exciting and rewarding functions in your group.

WHAT DOES PUBLICITY INCLUDE?

Not-for-profit organizations can learn a great deal from the for-profit sector in advertising and public relations. In fact, in recent years there have been a number of books written about marketing for nonprofit organizations. These have dealt with the four critical elements of selling an organization—product, price, promotion, and distribution.

For local committees involved in international exchange programs the most pertinent areas for marketing are product and promotion, although being able to explain pricing is often very useful. The question of how you distribute your service to your clients is seldom a problem, since your clients for the most part come to you.

Nevertheless, it is useful to focus on product and promotion. For purposes of our discussion, I will call these two areas "publicity to create awareness of your organization" and "publicity to promote specific events and activities." These are two distinctly different activities requiring different strategies, different techniques, and different campaigns.

PUBLICITY TO CREATE AWARENESS OF YOUR ORGANIZATION

As we have noted several times during this discussion of local committee functions, a clear understanding of your committee mission and objectives is critical to your success. It is not only important in organization planning and the recruitment of volunteers, as we have already suggested, but, as you will see in this chapter and the next, it is also crucial to your publicity and fund-raising campaigns.

With an increasing number of organizations involved in international activities today, you may be faced with the challenge of telling potential supporters and the public exactly what your organization does and how it is different from the "competition." While most of us do not believe that "competition" among not-for-profit organizations is necessary, it is a fact of life that when there are a number of organizations all seeking the same scarce resources (volunteers and funds), there is likely to be healthy competition. To turn your back on this is at best naïve and at worst irresponsible. You need to know how to tell your story in any case, and if another organization forces you to do it more succinctly, they are really doing you a service! (How's that for an optimistic approach to the situation?)

Every organization needs to plan an annual publicity campaign, just like an annual fund-raising campaign, volunteer recruitment campaign, host family recruitment campaign, and so on. The more these activities are planned on an annual basis, the more creative, organized, and forceful the results will be. In publicity, an *annual campaign for organization-awareness* focuses on telling the story about the following:

- your organization's mission and purpose

- your organization's objectives for the year

- the programs and activities of your organization

- the forms of support your organization needs

- the way people can support your organization

The main techniques used for this are a *brochure* and *newspaper* coverage. If you can get your local newspaper to agree to give you one general-purpose story each year, this will be something you can plan on. In fact, this is a good way to approach your local publisher or editor with a request for an "in-kind" contribution. This does not limit you in your ability to obtain additional space based on specific events or activities during the year. This you should be able to get on a competitive basis. General-interest reviews, however, are harder to get and usually take a targeted effort aimed at the particular media's decision-makers.

An organization *brochure* is the other component of an annual general publicity campaign. If you are president of a small chapter, you may feel that a brochure is too costly and unnecessary. I respectfully disagree on both counts.

First, the preparation of a brochure creates an excellent opportunity for your chapter to review the clarity of its mission and purpose and the degree to which all members in your organization are aware of and in agreement with your goals, objectives, and activities. Communicating what your organization is all about in writing in a limited space makes everyone think hard about exactly what you are trying to accomplish. You will find that you will achieve new insights and greater clarity in your ability to represent your organization.

Second, a brochure does not have to be costly. You should be able to receive help from your local printer on layout and design and perhaps even get an in-kind contribution or discount for the printing. While we will review specific techniques for preparing simple brochures in a moment, it should be noted here that one of the best forms of brochures for local work is a self-mailer that can also fit into a normal legal-size envelope if you want to enclose it in a letter. The simplest and cheapest form is a piece of 8½ × 11 paper, printed on both sides, and folded in thirds. This creates six sides to work with, is easy to fold, and requires little expense. Naturally, you can start at this point and become increasingly elaborate, depending upon your budget and what the competition is doing.

Your organization-awareness campaign should be planned in advance for the time during the year that you could benefit most from a general interest article. You can then request this far enough in advance that your local newspaper can plan on it. You should obviously try to get the newspaper to list a phone number where people can call for additional information, which is one of the many times that a brochure is useful to have on hand.

PUBLICITY IN SUPPORT OF SPECIAL EVENTS

Good publicity ideas are not hard to find, especially for an active organization working in international exchange. People are always interested in reading about international visitors or people from the community who have been selected to go abroad on exchange programs. In addition, there is a wide range of events that take place in most international exchange organizations that can compete favorably for space against other local events. Here are some:

News About Arriving and Departing Exchangees

The name and background of your expected international visitor—along with an interesting, unposed picture if available—is a good way to alert your community to a person's impending arrival. You might include an interview with the family who will be hosting the visitor to review their expectations and feelings as they anticipate their experience.

Of course, the visitor's arrival in the new community and reactions to new experiences provide interesting newsworthy opportunities. The less copy printed the better at this point, however, since the visitor may not be in a good position to give first impressions because of language, nervousness, or lack of perspective.

The planned departure of a student or group from the community for an exchange abroad is another opportunity for publicity. Many local newspapers are willing and eager to have a local student write back his impressions of his stay overseas. In other cases, special interest stories describing various aspects of life abroad are easy to place, especially if the lifestyle of the foreign country is markedly different from your local community's.

Involvement of Public Figures

Some communities have found that if a well-known person in town can be induced to speak to the press about the activities of your local chapter, more interest will be shown in your activities. The school superintendent, the mayor, or any prominent person who has been involved with your group is a good possibility.

Follow-up on Former Visitors

You should not miss the opportunity for publicity provided by a visit several years later by someone who once lived in your community as an international visitor. Many former foreign students, in particular, come back to see their host families, but seldom is anyone in the local chapter ready to use this chance for local publicity. All former host families should be alerted to the fact that they should contact the chapter if they expect a visit from someone who previously lived with them.

The angles in which newspapers are particularly interested are any observations the visitor has about changes in the community or comparisons of the community to their own once he returned home. The challenges of readjustment when they return to their home country after leaving your community are also full of rich possibilities if handled in a constructive manner. Finally, everyone likes to know that the visit of someone to their community resulted in some important learning opportunity. If you can get former visitors to articulate the impact of their stay in your community on their life, you are not only creating interesting reading, but also developing a case for future support of your organization!

Fund-raising and Other Events

Fund-raising activities (whether a car wash or an international dinner) also deserve publicity, not only to report on the results, but also in attracting support in advance. Your fund-raising people should work closely with your publicity coordinator in planning and scheduling fund-raising events that are not in competition with other local community events for media space or attendance. To do this requires some planning in advance (preferably on an annual basis) so that you can schedule your events for the most opportune time.

In cases where your events are not tied to fund-raising (plays, lectures, slide shows and international fairs), publicity can be a chief side benefit. In small- and medium-sized communities, there is always interest in reporting on functions that have been well attended and are of general community interest. If you plan to have three or four special events during the course of the year that you want covered, you should be able to accomplish this with some advance scheduling.

In *all* cases, it is best to accompany any article you send to the newspaper with a $5'' \times 7''$ or $8'' \times 10''$ black-and-white glossy of good quality. Weekly newspapers in particular are often looking for interesting pictures.

Special Events as Publicity

Publicity can be generated not only *in support of special events,* but an opportunity for public relations can become an event in itself. Examples of this include slide presentations to local civic and social organizations, placing a booth at local community functions like church bazaars and state fairs, and displays suitable for mounting in banks, libraries, schools, shopping malls, small retail shops, department stores, and other busy places in the community. Displays are an especially useful multipurpose medium. Enlarged photographs and blown-up type in a neat arrangement can create an eye-catching exhibit that can draw the public's attention to your programs and their purpose. Such displays are especially useful in connection with an "International Visitor Week," which might have been designated in your community by the mayor. In this way, you are not asking merchants to advertise your program permanently, but only to support the special week in your community dedicated to its purpose.

In the end, people's natural curiosity is your best guide to good publicity ideas. What would *you* be interested in reading about in your local newspaper or hearing about on your local radio and TV station? That is a good indicator of what others might be interested in also.

WORKING WITH PUBLIC MEDIA

You may be surprised at the number of *newspapers and magazines* that serve your community—some you may not have heard of before. Ask your library or local newspaper if you may see this year's edition of *Editor and Publisher Yearbook* (published by Editor and Publisher, Inc., 575 Lexington Avenue, New York, New York 10022). This will give you an up-to-date list of the publications in your area.

On the other hand, *television and radio* remain probably the most solid communication force in the United States. Millions of Americans regularly tune into one or the other, particularly during "wake up" and "drive home" periods. Talk shows are often looking for topics. An articulate spokesperson for your group can join an international visitor (provided the latter is relatively fluent in English) and turn their discussion into a fascinating program. It is usually not advisable, however, to let a foreign visitor carry a talk show alone, since there are some aspects of your group's work you can represent better than a person on the receiving end. A visitor also may be nervous and too inexperienced to remember such things as plugging hosting opportunities or other aspects of your organization's work that can be used to recruit additional support from such a program.

Television and radio information (including telephone numbers, program directors' names, locations of stations, the number of subscribers to cable TV operations, etc.) is included in another annual publication, *Broadcasting Yearbook* (published by Broadcasting Publications, Inc., 1735 De Sales St., N.W., Washington, D.C., 20036). Like the newspaper yearbook, this reference tool is expensive;

so check with a local radio or TV station or library and ask to borrow it.

If your organization is going to present a written news or feature release to newspapers or to radio and TV stations, a few basic pointers may be helpful. First, get the facts right. Second, keep it simple. Third, hand-deliver the message.

Facts

You can combine local items (how many foreign visitors have come to your community through your programs over the years; how old your program is) with worldwide information about your organization. Include the data as background for some news stories. Have a "basic fact sheet" about your organization as a one- or two-page handout for all media events. The important rule is to make sure the background information is factual and not editorialized. Editorializing is, for example, describing your organization as "one of the finest opportunities available today to meet people from other countries." While you may believe this very strongly, it is a judgment that can be disputed. Facts should be simple statements of indisputable information that the media can use as background for their own editorial assessments of your organization and its programs.

Simplicity

When writing for public consumption, it is important to keep your sentences short and ideas simple. You must assume that the person knows nothing about your organization and has little time to learn about you.

News writing calls for putting the most pertinent information at the beginning of a story. It should take only a couple of paragraphs for the reader to be able to answer the five cardinal questions applied to news items: Who? What? When? Where? and Why? And it is often legitimate to ask another question—How?

> Homemade ice cream proved a delightful way to end the Hometown International Festival yesterday . . .

This is not the opening of a news story that will win its way into an editor's heart! The main purpose of the festival, however, could well encourage her to give you some space in her paper. For example:

The Hometown Council for International Visitors announced at its monthly meeting yesterday that plans are set for the arrival of six teachers from India. Beginning March 1 for a period of one week the teachers will live with Hometown families and have a chance to observe classes at Hometown elementary and secondary schools. Special events have been arranged with faculty and students to compare schools in Hometown with schools in India.

"This is one of many interesting ways in which we try to enrich life in our community, by allowing people in Hometown to meet people from other parts of the world," said Ray Smith, the President of the Council for International Visitors. "We are always looking for people interested in helping us to host our visitors and attend our events. We look forward to a good turnout at our evening discussion with the teachers at the high school at 8:00 PM next Wednesday. The public is invited and it will be an excellent opportunity to meet our visitors and learn more about the work of our organization."

Thus, within two paragraphs, the news release presents the really important "what," and in addition includes facts about who, when, where, and at least some introductory comments about how interested people might become involved in the organization. By moving the pertinent information in a news story toward the beginning, you also conform to the "inverted-pyramid" style of journalistic communication. This simply means that if the story has to be reduced in size because there is not enough space in a newspaper for the entire article, the later paragraphs of the story can be deleted without jeopardizing the basic information included in the release.

This release also establishes a spokesperson for the Council. It is not always necessary to make your organization's president the exclusive voice of your organization, but it is dangerous to have two or more people talking to the press and saying different things. Usually, a good policy is to have one individual assigned to make comments for publication. Many times this is the publicity coordinator, who knows the kinds of angles editors are looking for and what kinds of comments are most "quotable."

Another example of how the "Who," "What," "How," and "Why" approach combines graphics with simplicity is included in Figure 7.

What better way to get someone's attention than by having a large

Figure 7

Welcome to the Friendship, MA, AFS Chapter Meeting

We would like to take this opportunity to introduce to you the programs and opportunities which AFS International/Intercultural Programs has to offer.

Who: Rina Brown—New Zealand
living in Westfield, MA
Jose Rodriguez—Mexico
living in Chatham, MA
Jane Garnet—Centerville, MA
AA to Argentina 1978
Ruth Newman—western MA
AFS area representative
John Mitchell—Providence, RI
AA to Italy 1967
field development consultant

What: It is our hope that Friendship
High will host two AFS students
in the fall of 1982 and that
Friendship sophomores, juniors
and seniors will have the opportunity to travel abroad to
live with a family for a
summer or a year.

How: By forming an AFS chapter in
Friendship, students and
community members will be
able to host foreign students.
And, students will have the
chance to participate in Americans Abroad, U.S.A. Program,
and the Short Term Exchange.

Why: To introduce a way of life to
a foreign student . . .
To provide new opportunities
to residents of Friendship . . .
To promote an exchange of
learning and teaching on new
international levels . . .
To encourage lasting
international friendships.

Contact: Susan Anderson, Friendship
High at 639-7214.

picture and an outline of the message you want to send them? It attracts their attention and saves their time so they don't have to go wading through paragraphs of material to find your message!

Hand Delivery

Once the release is completed, it should be brought to the media, since many times reporters want more substance and direct quotations to enhance a story. Being there is a way of showing your concern that the story be given more attention than the dozens of news releases that flood an editor's desk. It also gives you a chance to use some personal chemistry to persuade the editor to use your story.

It is critical that press personnel be encouraged to give full credit to your organization in articles. The use of vague terms such as "hospitality programs" or "exchange students" doesn't help establish your organization's image, especially if there are a number of organizations operating in the same field in your community. There is nothing more frustrating than to have a wonderful story appear about your organization's activities and not be identified by name as the group sponsoring the event!

These are some guidelines for dealing with the public media. The public media can be accessible and can be managed, but it takes someone in your organization who has exclusive responsibility for getting to know the press, radio and TV reporters, and editors, and who can develop some understanding of the "angles" they prefer, their deadlines and schedules, their basic layout and philosophy of presenting news, and the best ways for them to be approached. This is not hard to do, it just takes some time and thought. If you don't have a publicity coordinator—find one immediately! It's an enjoyable job and will be one of the best volunteer positions you have ever created for your organization.

PRIVATE MEDIA: DO IT YOURSELF!

If by now you are concerned that the only way you can get information disseminated about your organization is by depending on the perhaps somewhat fickle public media in your community, do not despair—there is another option.

There are all sorts of target audiences you can pinpoint and communicate with in ways which do not involve the public media at all. Figure 8 shows an example of a brochure aimed at school teachers by a group of mid-Ohio businessmen willing to speak on international affairs in local schools. This group used their own business advertising skills in developing a simple 8½ × 11″ one-page three-fold brochure to advertise their program. You can do the same for your own organization with very little trouble.

Your whole chapter, not just your publicity coordinator, needs to determine where you want to concentrate your annual public relations campaign. Many of them will have access to other community groups that can be targeted and approached through their own communication networks. Such potential targets include church organizations, local business associations, and groups interested in international travel as an adjunct to their primary activity.

For example, let us assume that your committee is interested in securing funds from the local chamber of commerce to help meet the expenses of a home hospitality program. The objective is given top priority by your committee. Your publicity coordinator, working with your fund-raising coordinator, seeks to develop a means of communication that will encourage support of your group by the chamber. This is how it might happen.

The publicity and fund-raising coordinators determine what to say and to whom to say it. The message in this case might be directed to all members of the chamber of commerce. The communication device could be a slide show to be presented at the chamber's monthly meeting, followed by distribution of a flyer about your group to all those who attend the meeting.

Your publicity coordinator can determine what tools are needed for both the slide presentation and to produce the flyer. You certainly have one or more camera enthusiasts on your committee who can provide the slides. As for producing a flyer, you need not spend more than thirty dollars to purchase the following items at your local art supply store:

- Three sheets of *rub-off headline type.* Letters are rubbed off these plastic sheets onto plain white paper.

- Two or three *art service books.* These are booklets of line-art drawings that can be used without fee to add visual image to your flyer.

Figure 8

Resources International Brochure

WHO ARE WE?

Resources International (RI) is an organization of volunteers from mid-Ohio: businessmen, researchers, world travelers, university professors and other community volunteers. We are eager to share our first-hand experience and knowledge of the world with you and your students.

HISTORY

On February 1, 1977, a meeting of the Board of Trustees of the International Council of Mid-Ohio was held to bring together committee chairpeople with their ideas. Dr. Chad Alger of Ohio State University,

chairman of the program committee, reported a promising project, development of an array of international resource people for the area schools. The International Council of Mid-Ohio is now the Columbus Council on World Affairs and the promising project is Resources International.

TOPICS

Sports
Education
Foreign Policy
Arts and Literature
History and Archeology
Social and Economic Problems
Government and Politics
Culture and Family Life
Business Practices
Health Care
Religion

in

AREAS OF THE WORLD

Africa
Caribbean

Soviet Union
Southeast Asia
North and South America
Mexico and Central America
Eastern and Western Europe
Australia and New Zealand
Middle East
East Asia

WE CAN HELP YOU

- Provide curriculum enrichment.
- Enlarge the educational experience of your students.
- Bring the excitement of world affairs into your classroom.
- Help your classes keep up with current international developments.

ISSUES

Population
World Hunger
Uses of the Oceans
Environment/Ecology
Arms Control and Disarmament
Problems of the Developing Nations
Energy and Diminishing

Resources
Cultural Differences
Human Rights

WE WILL

- Come to your school and speak to your class.
- Show slides and display artifacts.
- Consult with you privately about program and curriculum development.
- Act as informal advisors.
- Arrange educational experiences in the community.
- Increase exposure to other cultures and to people involved in world affairs.
- Help students comprehend the many ways their daily lives are intertwined with those throughout the world.

All this at no cost for grade levels, K-12

Resources International (RI) is a service of the Columbus Council on World Affairs.

Art work donated by Jerry Smith. Brochure funded by The Miriam C. Wollam Fund.

- Other helpful tools:

  a *T-square,* used to make sure type is straight when pasting up the flyer

  rubber cement, a type of adhesive that permits you to move lines of type around after the glue has set (almost a necessity!)

  safety-edge razor blades for fast trimming

  a *nonreproducing blue pencil* to make marks and write instructions that will not be picked up when the flyer paste-up is photographed for reproduction

  a *typewriter* with clean type and a fresh ribbon

  ruler

  scissors

  several sheets of *plain white paper*

A good flyer combines art, headlines, and body copy into a communication form that grabs the reader's attention (see example in Figure 9). If you are unsure how the flyer should be designed, talk with the high school art teacher, or a newspaper advertising specialist in your community. Generally, a review of sample magazine ads will provide you with many creative ideas.

When you have your paste-up ready, your flyer can be reproduced by various methods.

Photocopy

You may use any good quality copying machine, although this process is more expensive than other production methods when large quantities are needed.

Figure 9

A Finished Flyer

Ready to be reproduced through electronic stencil or offset. Colored paper can be used to give a more striking appearance.

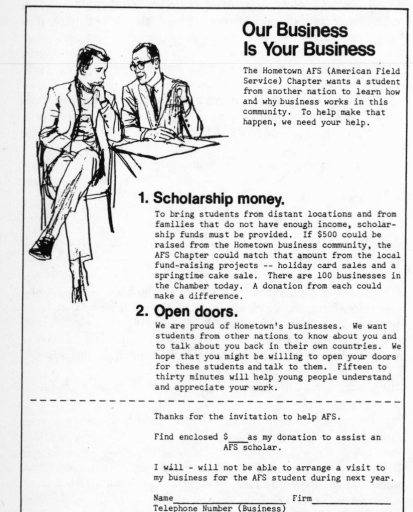

Our Business Is Your Business

The Hometown AFS (American Field Service) Chapter wants a student from another nation to learn how and why business works in this community. To help make that happen, we need your help.

1. Scholarship money.

To bring students from distant locations and from families that do not have enough income, scholarship funds must be provided. If $500 could be raised from the Hometown business community, the AFS Chapter could match that amount from the local fund-raising projects -- holiday card sales and a springtime cake sale. There are 100 businesses in the Chamber today. A donation from each could make a difference.

2. Open doors.

We are proud of Hometown's businesses. We want students from other nations to know about you and to talk about you back in their own countries. We hope that you might be willing to open your doors for these students and talk to them. Fifteen to thirty minutes will help young people understand and appreciate your work.

- -

Thanks for the invitation to help AFS.

Find enclosed $____ as my donation to assist an AFS scholar.

I will - will not be able to arrange a visit to my business for the AFS student during next year.

Name_____ Firm_____
Telephone Number (Business)_____

Offset

Modern printing firms are converting to offset presses that make copy reproduction much easier and cheaper than other printing methods. When large quantities of flyers are needed (more than a hundred), or photographs are an integral part of your layout, offset is a good choice. Small print shops are glad to provide price estimates. To do this, the printer needs to know—in addition to the required quantity and color and grade of paper and ink—whether the flyer is to be delivered to you folded or flat, whether it will be printed on one or two sides, and whether collating/binding will be necessary. Many schools have print shops that can handle this kind of work. A call to your high school administrative office may result in considerable savings for your group.

You will notice that the flyer included in our example contains a tear-off section. This is a very useful way of getting additional mileage from your flyer and also of measuring its impact.

Printed paper alone, however, will not meet your fund-raising or any other need. Flyers and all print media are merely supportive materials for the personal visits and telephone calls that in the end will bring the results you are looking for. By combining several forms of communication (slides, discussions, flyers, brochures, news articles, and phone calls) you can develop an effective communications program, which will aid you in meeting your organization's objectives.

A WORD ABOUT "THE BIG THREE" RESOURCE BUILDERS

Publicity can be fun. Certainly it is one of the keys to your committee's success. Be sure to recruit someone for the job who is enthusiastic and looks forward to doing it. This person will be one of the three critical people building the human and financial resources necessary for your organization to succeed.

In the end, your resource base is dependent upon cooperation between "The Big Three" resource builders—your membership chairperson (for human resources), your fund-raising chairperson (for financial resources), and your publicity coordinator (for the case statement, the outreach, and the support of your recruiting and fund-raising efforts). If these three people see themselves as a team with an integrated task, working under the supervision of the chapter president and within the annual goals, programs, and objectives of your chapter, you should produce some exciting and productive ideas, acquiring the resources that make it possible for your program to grow and flourish.

We have examined two of these three areas, in Chapter 5 and this chapter. Let us turn now to the third key resource-building job necessary for your organization's health and development—fund-raising.

For Further Study

Kotler, Philip. *Marketing for Nonprofit Organizations.* 2nd ed. Englewood Cliffs, N.J.: Prentice Hall, Inc., 1975.

Levine, Howard and Carol Levine. *Effective Public Relations for Community Groups.* New York: Association Press, 1969.

Maddalena, Lucille A. *A Communications Manual for Nonprofit Organizations.* New York: American Management Association, 1980.

Montana, Patrick J. *Marketing in Nonprofit Organizations.* New York: American Management Association, 1978.

Fund-raising Keys

7

Historically, fund-raising has consisted of anything from passing church collection plates to soliciting major gifts from foundations. In the United States today, fund-raising has become a well-developed and sophisticated art form.

With the multiplication of causes and the cutback in government funding for many domestic programs that had been government supported since the 1960s, there is increasing competition for the scarce resources available from the private sector. As a result, the professional expertise of the country has begun to focus on more sophisticated ways to raise money, computer technology is being applied, and this area, as an area of scarcity in a free enterprise system, has now become subject to the throes of competitive creativity to find the best way to raise funds necessary for not-for-profit operations.

Since the survival of your group and many other local not-for-profit groups in your community depends upon fund-raising ideas and activities, your fund-raising approach today must be more systematically planned, better developed, better organized, and presented more persuasively than ever before.

HOW TO BEGIN

The first step necessary in any fund-raising effort is to review your organization and its mission, as we suggested in Chapter 3. Is your organization still relevant to the needs of your community? Are you doing something that is perceived as worthy and helpful to the people of the community? If you have let your organization falter in its basic mission, you can stop now in your fund-raising plan and go back to your basic organizational planning. Nothing is more difficult than raising money for an organization that is not perceived as relevant to local needs! Unless you have this issue in hand, you will have an uphill, if not an impossible struggle to sustain your funding base.

If you conclude that your organization is meeting felt community needs and that it is recognized as an effective contributor to the community, then you are in a position to begin fund-raising.

DEVELOPING THE "CASE STATEMENT"

By now you are probably very tired of hearing me say that you need to articulate the mission, goals, and objectives of your organization, but I am going to say it anyway. Just as in planning your programs, recruiting volunteers, and seeking publicity, if you don't know what you're doing and can't articulate it in a forceful and persuasive manner, then you will not be able to attract the resources (including money) necessary to maintain and develop your organization.

In fund-raising, the process is called developing a "case statement." A case statement should not be very different from your original mission statement and the statement of objectives for the forthcoming year. If you have done your homework on planning, as discussed in Chapter 3, you have already done one of the most important parts of your fund-raising campaign—the development of a case for your organization.

Professional fund-raisers will tell you that a "case statement" can be contained in a special brochure or just be set down in three or four succinctly typewritten pages. In it, you should clearly state the following:

- the *history and mission* of your organization

- the *need* your group is trying to meet in your community

- what *programs* you have planned for the year to meet this need

- why your group is *uniquely suited* to carry this out

- who else *supports* your work

- what it will *cost*

- what the reader can do to *help*

You might consider using a pie chart to portray your income and expenditures graphically.

In preparing your case, keep these factors in mind:

THE CASE SHOULD BE BIGGER THAN YOUR ORGANIZATION

Your presentation will be stronger if you focus on the value of your organization for world understanding than if you focus immediately on specific funds for a specific project. This is why you should start with your statement of mission.

YOUR CASE SHOULD BE PRAGMATIC AND IDEALISTIC

Having just been encouraged to emphasize the broader idealistic aspects of your organization, you should not, nevertheless, forget that ultimately many people will give (or volunteer, remember Chapter 5?) for a combination of idealistic and pragmatic reasons. In other words, you need to make the case in terms of the relationship of broader world issues to your community and its needs.

A SENSE OF IMMEDIACY OF NEED IS A PREREQUISITE

I am not implying that you should give the impression that your organization is on the verge of bankruptcy! On the contrary, fund-raising is easiest for organizations that are perceived to be well-run and financially responsible. You should, however, be able to demonstrate that without adequate funding certain programs that are badly needed by the community may not be able to be carried out. If people believe you can carry on without their help, they'll be inclined to let you do just that!

CURRENT NEED AND CONTRIBUTION IS ESSENTIAL

Your emphasis must be on the present and the future, not the past. It is, of course, important to outline your past achievements and to demonstrate that you are a solid organization with proven capacity to deliver. Your ability to attract funds, however, will in most cases not be for what you have accomplished in the past, but for your capacity to meet needs of the future. Therefore, don't spend too much time talking about how much you have done—focus on how much you will do!

YOUR CASE MUST BE SUPPORTABLE

It must be able to withstand the scrutiny of business or financial reviews. You should be sure your financial projections of need are sound and well presented, and you should be secure in your ability to demonstrate you have the organizational capacity to carry out the plans you have set forth.

YOUR CASE SHOULD AFFECT AS MANY POTENTIAL SUPPORTERS AS POSSIBLE

Obviously, you want to have as large a "target population" for your appeal as you can. You should, therefore, be attentive when writing your case to how you can make it attractive to as many different interest groups in your community as possible.

YOUR CASE MUST BE EXPRESSED CLEARLY AND CONCISELY

Use subheadings, bulleted indentations, and a layout that is easily readable and memorable.

If you follow these guidelines you'll have a "case statement" that will give you a strong start in raising the funds you need.

DEVELOPING THE CAMPAIGN

When you have a good case prepared, either for general release or for your own internal committee planning and use, you will be ready to plan a financial campaign to meet your projected needs.

Like everything done well, it takes concern, time, and effort to organize a successful financial campaign. For this reason your fund-raising chairperson should be prepared to recruit as many people as possible to help. Fund-raising, perhaps more than any other volunteer activity, is a team effort.

One strategy that has been used successfully by AFS chapters is called the GAP plan. It is aimed at bridging the fund-raising gap between your hopes for your program and your financial resources. GAP stands for:

G = Goals

A = Assignments and Authority

P = People

With these three components, seemingly insurmountable fund-raising needs have often been met. Let's see how it works.

Goals

I have stressed a goal-directed approach to the management of your volunteer organization since the first chapter of this book. This is because it has proven the most effective way of organizing and motivating people in both the for-profit and not-for-profit area over the last thirty years.

Ever since the well-known management writer, Peter Drucker, developed the concept of Management by Objectives (MBO) in the 1950s, organizations and managers have been setting goals and working to achieve new levels of accomplishment. You will also remember from our discussion of achievement motivation in Chapter 5 that goal-setting was one of the prime characteristics of people with a high need for (and record of) achievement.

A critical part of the GAP plan involves plotting realistic, but challenging objectives (also a characteristic of high achievers, remember?). To do this, you must have your programs for the year as clearly and carefully outlined as possible. In this way, you can examine the financial costs associated with each program and from them develop a budget for your organization for the year.

The example shown in Figure 10 describes how the Hometown Sister Cities Committee went about its yearly fund-raising. Note that all the activities for the year have been planned ahead and a financial cost has been assigned to each. It is assumed that the figures represent only out-of-pocket expenses, those that volunteers will not cover either through contribution of time or individual funds. It is important, however, to point out in your fund-raising the amount of volunteer service and contribution that will be made toward any effort.

One area you should be particularly cognizant of is "in-kind" contributions. I would suggest that if you anticipate two hundred dollars in printing expenses, for example, you include that sum in your budget presentation, but then attempt to have someone contribute it. This is better than eliminating it from your budget in the *hope* that it will be contributed. There are two reasons for this approach. First, the person making the contribution likes to feel that he or she is helping the organization meet a real need for which you would otherwise have had to pay. And second, you have a more dependable budget if you begin by being realistic about the costs you will incur, rather than "hoping" some of them away.

The first principle of managing a not-for-profit organization, however, is always to ask for *everything* to be donated. That way, you pay only what is necessary and can't be gotten by donation.

Assignments and Authority

Once financial costs have been determined and the fund-raising goals associated with them have been established, you are ready to assess the most likely sources of income for each project.

In some cases, you will decide that you can go to a particular source for "project support" on one of your activities; that is, approach someone or some local business to completely support one of your events or one of your exchangees. In return for this support, you would obviously be willing to give the person whatever publicity he or she might want. Be careful about how this offer is made, however, because the last thing some very wealthy people want is any publicity about their giving, sometimes from a sense of modesty, and in other

Figure 10

Hometown Sister Cities Committee: Fund-raising

Hometown is a community of 15,000 people, ten retail stores, and an electronics firm. It has three churches, a number of civic groups, a secondary school, and an international relations club.

The local Sister Cities chapter is planning to host one high school student for the AFS program, offer home hospitality for ten fourth-year medical student professionals visiting the community during the year, and send five civic leaders abroad for short professional visits. In addition, it will host a choral group from its Sister City and will send about six local Girl and Boy Scouts abroad.

Predictable Budget Needs:

1. Membership dues to Sister Cities International. $ 100

2. Scholarship fee for AFS student from Sister City. $ 850

3. Home hospitality for medical students for three weeks. $1,000

4. Five civic leaders to be sent abroad for two weeks. $2,500

5. Home hospitality for choral group from Sister City. $ 500

6. Six Boy Scouts and Girl Scouts to Sister City. $ 300

Fund-Raising Goals:

1. *Dues.* To be received from individuals, families, local organizations and businesses, and other benefactors as a result of letter appeal. $1,150

2. *Business Solicitation.* Team member to raise an average of $100 per business or industry in community. $1,000

3. *School / Civic Organizations.* Given a dozen groups plus three churches and a school with an international club, this team member should be able to raise an average of $100 per group. $1,600

4. *Community Activities.* Three events during the year, as follows:
    a. *October.* Communitywide door-to-door solicitation by high school International Club and other committee members to sell "Sister City Friendship Bonds." $1,000
    b. *December.* Christmas choral concert by visiting choir from Sister City. $ 500

Figure 10 Continued

Hometown Sister Cities Committee:
Fund-raising

Predictable Budget Needs:	Fund-Raising Goals:
7. Local administrative and operating expenses for publicity and other general activities. $ 500	c. *April.* Community Service Workday with Boy Scouts and Girl Scouts to help raise funds for Sister City Program. $ 500
	TOTAL MINIMUM
TOTAL NEEDS $5,750	REVENUE $5,750

instances to avoid being inundated with requests by other causes if it is known that they have generously supported one.

When you know the most likely sources of income for each activity, you will also know how much additional funding you must raise for those activities and for the administrative overhead which may not be covered by project funds. In many cases, this overhead may be your entire budget if you do not see any way to make a special appeal to someone in your community for designated support.

When you have finished targeting your income sources, you are ready to assign responsibility and authority to a team of individuals who will undertake to raise funds from each of the target groups. As part of each assignment, state the target group and amount of money each person is responsible for raising and set a deadline for soliciting the money. In this way, your fund-raisers will know what your expectations are and what responsibilities they are assuming.

One of the keys to raising relatively large amounts of money in small communities is to break down a large budget—like $5,750—into smaller components, as has been done in Figure 10. It is much less overwhelming for a new member of your fund-raising team to be asked to raise $1,000 than for her to feel the overall responsibility for raising $5,750.

People

You may also find that you will be able to attract a local civic leader to raise funds from a particular sector of the community during a limited drive, whereas such a person might not be willing to serve on the fund-raising committee over an entire year. This raises the question of how you get people interested and willing to take on fund-raising responsibility.

Fund-raising does not have to be the most painful job in your organization. If you follow some of the guidelines in this chapter it can be a very manageable task. It *is* important, however, that the *chapter* feel responsible for the fund-raising effort at some level and that as many chapter members as possible agree to contribute time to the fund-raising effort *in addition* to whatever other responsibilities they have. In this way, the fund-raising chairperson will not feel the onus of having to achieve the financial targets single-handedly.

In addition, however, you should have a fund-raising team specifically designated to raise funds. This team should be no fewer than three people and probably not more than eight. Each member should understand the mission and case statement and feel committed to the organization and excited about the plans for the forthcoming year. It might be useful for your chapter president to meet with the team at its first meeting and be sure that everyone is clear about what those plans are.

In our example of the Hometown Sister Cities Chapter in Figure 10, a team of four people would be appropriate. Each person could take responsibility for one of the four major fund-raising strategies to be used during the campaign. These are membership dues, business solicitations, school functions, and community activities.

Each person charged with responsibility for a target group should already be a member of that group. Your fund-raising chairperson should be particularly well-organized, able to help people plan their activities, and willing to follow up and monitor the implementation of their plans. You may want to let this person recruit three other people, or you may offer to help in identifying and approaching other people to be on the team.

While the GAP plan for fund-raising will make the job easier, raising money will still require some concentrated attention during a limited time period. The fund-raising chairperson should keep both the committee and the team moving toward their goals. At the end of the campaign, when the goals have been met, a recognition dinner, party, or some other nonwork event should be organized to express the committee's gratitude, not only to the major donors, but also to the people who provided leadership on the campaign.

RAISING FUNDS FROM COMMUNITY PROJECTS

A word should be added here about special fund-raising projects. Community projects have proven to be of enormous value to many local volunteer groups for three basic reasons:

1. They can often be combined with an excellent public relations drive to bring your organization's work before the eyes of the community.

2. They involve large groups of people and, therefore, give many members an opportunity to contribute their time to a project that can be fun and meaningful.

3. They do not require a large amount of money from any one person, but instead depend upon a quantity of small donors rather than the size of individual gifts for their success.

These obvious advantages allow community projects to do more for your organization than merely produce income. They can be used for membership promotions, motivating current volunteers, and gaining the support of local officials.

Figure 11

101 Fund-raising Ideas

1. Fashion shows.
2. School vending machines.
3. Book fairs.
4. Holiday greetings through the newspapers.
5. Annual art shows.
6. Pancake breakfasts.
7. AFS discounts (merchants' cards).
8. Selling decorated eggs from door to door.
9. Taking pictures of school children.
10. School directory sales.
11. Barbecues.
12. Coin cards, canisters.
13. International luncheons.
14. Quick-food coupons.
15. Tennis tournaments.
16. Zip-code book sales.
17. Selling postcards of AFS students.
18. Contests.
19. Sale of AFS decals.
20. Donations from the PTA.
21. Halloween spook house.
22. Raffles: quilts, trips, services, sides of beef, used cars, cash.

Figure 11 Continued

101 Fund-raising Ideas

---

23. Birthday-calendar sales.
24. Doughnut and hot-chocolate sales in the morning at school.
25. Painting house numbers on curbs.
26. International cookbook sales.
27. Bike-a-thons.
28. Donations from businesses.
29. Plant-clipping sales.
30. A mile of pennies (c. $635).
31. Pecan sales.
32. Bus trips for your community.
33. Craft fairs; bazaars.
34. International-doll sales.
35. Door-to-door solicitations.
36. Radiothons.
37. Magazine sales.
38. Donations from service clubs.
39. Community sings.
40. Concessions at school events.
41. Donations from school-locker deposits.
42. Walkathons.
43. Lights on for AFS.
44. Student-faculty competitions.
45. Carnivals.
46. Hero-sandwich sales.
47. International dinners (catered and potluck).
48. Travel-film series.
49. Rummage sales.
50. Appeal letters.
51. Gym-bag sales.
52. Class competitions.
53. Donations from the United Fund.
54. Dime-a-dip suppers.
55. Foundation grants.
56. Light-bulb sales.
57. Dances (two-generation dances and dance marathons).
58. AFS bond sales.
59. Flower sale; geranium sale.
60. Bottle and paper drives.
61. Talent shows.
62. Donations from retailers.
63. Chapter dues.
64. Taking your school's census.
65. Bake sales.
66. Student workdays.
67. Product testing for companies.
68. Progressive dinners.
69. Snow-cone sales.
70. Ice cream socials.
71. Car washes.
72. School-calendar sales.
73. Pizza sales.
74. Phonothons.
75. Auctions.
76. Theater benefits.
77. Spaghetti suppers.
78. Casino nights.
79. Concerts.
80. Citrus-fruit sales.
81. Cocktail parties.
82. Holiday-card sales.
83. International desserts.
84. Bridge parties and card parties.
85. Bingo.
86. AFS-button sales.
87. House tours.
88. Candy sales.
89. Wine- and cheese-tasting parties.
90. Donkey baseball.
91. Penny Wednesdays.
92. Block parties; street fairs.
93. Matching donations.
94. "Name" attractions and entertainment.
95. "Battle of the bands."
96. Key contests.
97. Balloon races.
98. Community musicals.
99. Taking a company's inventory.
100. Babysitting proceeds.
101. AFS-notepaper sales.

What do all these ideas have in common?

They have all been used by AFS chapters successfully to raise money. Every idea will not work in every community with every chapter. Pick one that is right for you.

Figure 11 lists 101 ideas for community fund-raising projects. You certainly can add others from your own experience, but see if there are any new ideas there that might be useful for you.

SEEKING GRANTS FROM LOCAL FOUNDATIONS OR LARGE CORPORATIONS

Since appealing to foundations and large corporations is not standard practice for local volunteer groups, I did not include this approach in the general fund-raising campaign strategy I have just described. One reason why groups do not normally tackle such sources of income is that they tend not to know exactly how to approach these rather more sophisticated (and beleaguered!) financial contributors.

If you are interested in approaching local foundations or major corporations for support, there are a number of guidelines to follow. These are explored below under research, approach, and (most important of all) "waiting."

RESEARCH

If you are interested in discovering whether your community has any foundations to which you might appeal or any large corporations that make funds available from a corporate foundation, you should consult the *Foundation Directory* (New York: The Foundation Center, 1981) in your local library. This directory lists over 5,000 foundations that give a total of $25,000 or more during the course of a year. Listed by state are the names of the foundations, their addresses, the names of the donors who established them, the purpose of their giving, financial information about them, and, most important, the names of officers and trustees whom you can contact for further information.

For corporations in your area, you can consult a study undertaken awhile ago by The Conference Board in New York City entitled *American Business Support for International Public Service Activities.*

It is somewhat out-of-date (published in the early seventies), but it will give you an idea of the kinds of corporations that support international activities and the kind of projects they are attracted to.

A review of these two publications should quickly tell you whether the particular foundation or corporation you are interested in makes grants for education or cultural activities or for the exchange of persons. You will find that many foundations rather narrowly limit the purposes for which they are willing to provide assistance. Be sure to familiarize yourself in advance with the foundation's objectives, policies, and resources. Failure to do this is one of the most common mistakes made by people who venture into this area for the first time. As a result they waste a great deal of their time and the time of the foundation executives they visit.

If you have any questions regarding whether or not a foundation or corporation is interested in your area, it is better to visit them than to merely telephone them. It is always easier for them to tell you over the phone that they are not interested, thereby precluding your having an opportunity to persuade them about the attractiveness of your work.

APPROACH

Once you have identified a foundation or corporation that clearly does make grants within your area of need, you should attempt to get an appointment with the foundation executive. In most cases, you will want to visit with the foundation executive before you develop a specific proposal, in order to ensure that you are taking the right approach or following any guidelines the foundation may have. If you choose this tactic, however, you should still have some need in mind for your meeting so that you can test the willingness of the foundation to consider your project. You should never go to a foundation executive and ask "What are you interested in funding?" Interest in funding will come from something within the foundation's purpose that strikes the executive as worthwhile. Your job is to prove to him that you have something worthwhile!

When approaching a foundation executive, it is to your advantage to have somebody in your organization who knows one of the foundation's officers or trustees personally. This person can not only assist you in developing a strategy for funding, but also should help in setting up an appointment and if possible accompany you to your meeting.

In every possible instance, your presentation should be made in person. You should not just send a proposal to a foundation or corporation "cold." In some cases where you feel you know that the foundation's interest in your organization is strong, you may want to send a proposal in advance of your meeting, requesting an appointment to discuss the specific details. In most cases, however, you will want to meet with the official *before* you run the risk of submitting a proposal that may be outside of the current foundation funding guidelines. There is nothing more disastrous than requesting $500 from a foundation that never gives grants of less than $5,000. On the other hand, it is equally silly to ask a foundation or corporation for $5,000 when they never give more than $1,000.

You will find that most local community foundations and large corporations give grants in the $500-to-$2,500 range. This is because they are spreading limited resources around to many different local organizations, rather than concentrating their funds of major grants in a limited number of areas. This is particularly true of corporate foundations, for whom a giving program many times is an extension of their general community-relations program, rather than a foundation in the true sense of the word. They have neither the staff nor the time to evaluate large complex projects and certainly do not have the funds to support many of these. As a result, you will find that many of your largest international corporations give small gifts of $1,000-$2,500 to a wide range of organizations.

Finally, if you anticipate requesting annual support, it is inadvisable to count on more than $1,000 to $1,500. Corporations are increasingly limiting their support to three years, with a break before allowing you to apply again. All these steps are being taken by corporations that have found themselves overwhelmed by requests for the limited funds they have available. In order to spread them around as fairly as possible, they have had to develop ways of turning down good causes without incurring the wrath of local community leaders whose support they need.

THE WAIT

After you have submitted your proposal there is little that you can do to hasten its processing. Most foundations have boards of trustees who meet one, two, three, or four times a year to review proposals and make grants. You should find out from your interview at the foundation when it might be brought for board review. In this way you will know approximately when you might be able to count on an answer to your request. It is standard practice to request such information and the foundation representative will be able to give it to you. In this way, you will be able to plan contingency fund-raising projects should your request be turned down.

One final note: You should not be disappointed if you fail to receive a favorable response to your first request. Professional fund-raisers frequently receive a positive response to only one out of every seven to ten proposals they submit to foundations and corporations. Most professionals will tell you, however, to resubmit the proposal again next year in the hope of receiving more favorable consideration. You should be aware that when you move into foundation and large corporate solicitation, you are entering a highly competitive field, which may require a great deal of work before you obtain any substantive results.

ACHIEVING FUND–RAISING SUCCESS

As noted earlier, the GAP plan is based on the characteristics of achievement motivation we discussed in Chapter 5. You also may recall that achievement-motivated people respond best to situations in which they:

- can take personal responsibility for their actions, depending more on talents and skills for success than on chance

- can take a risk that is moderate and proportionate to their resources for coping with it

- can plan their future with specific goals

- can receive concrete feedback on their performance

This is in many ways the key to achieving fund-raising success. The GAP plan breaks the solicitation of a large amount of money down into specific, small, achievable tasks for which people can take responsibility, which are moderate in risk, which can be approached in a planned manner, and from which there can be specific feedback concerning the success of the project. This is the essence of an effective fund-raising campaign.

Finally, we must not overlook the fact that fund-raising should be as much fun as you can make it. That may seem odd, because so many people see fund-raising as a necessary evil. But this isn't so. Many studies have shown that the need to raise money has been one of the primary forces keeping groups together. Fund-raising gives people a reason to work together on projects and many have fun in the process. There is a great sense of satisfaction from carrying out a successful fund-raising campaign that can give people as much of a sense of accomplishment as the program of the organization itself.

If your fund-raising is not *fun* raising also, you should go back to Chapter 4 and review the health of your organization—you may have just caught a cold!

For Further Study

Broce, Thomas E. *Fund Raising: The Guide to Raising Money from Private Sources.* Oklahoma: University of Oklahoma Press, 1979.

Dermer, Joseph. *How to Write Successful Foundation Presentations.* New York: Public Service Materials Center, 1972.

Flanagan, Joan. *The Grassroots Fundraising Book: How to Raise Money in a Community.* Washington, D.C.: Youth Project, 1555 Connecticut Avenue, 1977.

_____. *The Successful Volunteer Organization.* Chicago: Contemporary Books, 1971, Chapters 12 and 13.

Kurzig, Carol. *Foundation Fundamentals: A Guide for Grantseekers.* New York: The Foundation Center, 1980.

Leibert, Edwin R. and Bernice E. Sheldon. *Handbook of Special Events for Nonprofit Organizations: Tested Ideas for Fundraising and Public Relations.* New York: Association Press, 1972.

Sheppard, William W. *Annual Giving Idea Book.* Plymouth Meeting, Pa.: The Fund Raising Institute, 1972.

White, Virginia P. *Grants: How to Find Out About Them and What to Do Next.* New York: Plenum Press, 1975.

Financial Accounting and Control | 8

This chapter focuses on budgeting, accounting, controlling, and cash management, since these are primary concerns of every local organization treasurer.[1] Before we get into these areas, however, let's start with the basic question most laymen ask about the subject: "Why bother to keep books at all; we're just a small organization?"

Joan Flanagan, in her book, *The Successful Volunteer Organization,* lists the following ways in which your organization can benefit from a clear accounting system, no matter how small your budget.[2] You need an accounting system because with it you can:

- Know where your money is now.

- Know where your money went.

- Know the sources of your money, so you know where to go back for more.

- Tell the people who gave you money last year exactly what you did with it. Since the best people to ask for money are the people who have already given you money, clear records make that task easier.

- Tell members how much it costs to run your program, what they get for their dues, and why they should continue to pay them.

- Accurately estimate how much money you will need next month or next year.

- Be confident that all the money is going where it is supposed to go.

- Have clear and accurate information when you have to fill out annual financial reports.

- Make it possible for a large group of people to share in the ownership of the organization.

Now that you know why you are in the accounting business, let's look at some of the technicalities.

THE DIFFERENCE BETWEEN BUDGETING, ACCOUNTING, AND CONTROLLING

It will probably be helpful to begin by clarifying the relationship among budgeting, accounting, and controlling. You may remember that in Chapter 3 we discussed the budgeting process as it was linked to planning. In fact, it is easiest to think of all three functions— budgeting, accounting, and controlling—in terms of planning, implementation, and evaluation.

Simply stated, *budgeting* is your plan for allocating funds that you intend to spend in the future; *accounting* is the recording of receipts and expenditures as they occur; and *controlling* is the process of evaluating your receipts and expenditures against your budget to determine whether or not you are operating within your financial plans and resources.

Maintaining financial control of your organization is one of the most important aspects of management. By this I do not mean control in terms of decision-making power, but control in maintaining an overview of your organization's directions, and the degree to which you are proceeding according to plan. While there are obviously program components to this monitoring and control process, the financial aspects are even more crucial. Without good financial controls, you may never have the opportunity to achieve your program objectives.

GOOD ACCOUNTING FOR YOUR OWN PROTECTION

Most small and medium-size not-for-profit organizations keep their accounts on a cash basis. Under this system, the only time a transaction is recorded is when cash has been received or expended. A simple checkbook is often all that is needed to keep your records. When financial statements are required, your treasurer just summarizes the transactions from the checkbook stubs. This may sound almost too easy, but a checkbook can be an adequate substitute for formal bookkeeping records, provided a complete description of each receipt and payment is recorded.

Figure 12 is a statement showing cash receipts, cash payments, and cash balance for the Hometown committee of Sister Cities that we worked with in the last chapter. Since receivables and payables are not recognized in cash-basis accounting (this is known as accrual accounting), a typical cash-basis balance sheet contains only cash that has been received or paid out.

As a result, Figure 12 contains transactions for the twelve-month period ending August 31. Every effort should be made to pay all bills before year-end to assure that the cash-basis statements provide as accurate a picture of the organization's financial situation as possible.

BUDGET COMPARISON

One of the first principles to remember when preparing financial statements is that they are a communications vehicle. The purpose is to present as clearly and intelligibly as possible a picture of the financial position of your organization. One way to do this is to provide the reader with a point of comparison to help evaluate the current situation. This could be a comparison with the same time last year or with last month or with the budget as in Figure 12. The important thing is that the reader be given some additional information with which to judge whether the figures present a good picture or one requiring action to correct a situation that is off-target. For local volunteer efforts whose programs change from year to year, it is unlikely that comparisons on a year-to-year basis will be as helpful as budget versus actual statements.

Figure 12

Hometown Sister Cities Committee: Cash Statement

Receipts and Cash Payments, September 1, 19—
Through August 31, 19—

Receipts:		Actual	Budget
1. Dues		$1,127	$1,150
2. Business solicitation		1,125	1,000
3. School civic organizations		1,430	1,600
4. Community activities		2,242	2,000
a. October, door-to-door	1,120		
b. December, Christmas choir	580		
c. April, Community Service Workday	542		
Total Receipts		$5,924	$5,750
Payments:			
1. Membership dues to Sister Cities International		$ 100	$ 100
2. Scholarship fee for AFS student from sister city		850	850
3. Home hospitality for medical students—3 weeks		935	1,000
4. Sending 5 civic leaders abroad—2 weeks		2,470	2,500
5. Hospitality for choral group from sister city		625	500
6. Sending 6 Boy Scouts and Girl Scouts to sister city		290	300
7. Local administrative and operating expenses		460	500
Total Payments		$5,730	$5,750
Excess of cash receipts over disbursements		194	—0—
Cash balance, September 1, 19—		47	—0—
Cash balance, August 31, 19—		$241	

Most local organizations have no investments, fixed assets or other funds that require statements of income, expenditures, and changes in fund balances. The accounting procedures for these statements are somewhat more complicated. Should you have any additional factors that require you to operate on an accrual basis or to have more than a checkbook accounting need, there are a number of references at the end of this chapter that you can consult for more sophisticated approaches.

CASH CONTRIBUTIONS

Thus far, we have dealt only with the form of accounting and not with the actual recording of cash receipts and expenditures. Of all cash receipts, cash contributions comprise most local volunteer organizational income. Normally, contributions pose few problems, being *unrestricted* for current use. Unrestricted donations are cash receipts to be used for whatever purposes you need them.

Occasionally, however, your group may receive a *restricted* contribution applicable for current operating purposes or for future purposes through an endowment fund. Endowment gifts are rare in local volunteer groups. Other restricted gifts are limited to some specific purpose. As we noted in the last chapter, you may have approached someone to underwrite a particular aspect of your program, such as a student scholarship. In such a case, when you receive this money, you must note that it is restricted for this purpose. The use of restricted donations cannot be changed by your organization, including your board. If you want to use the money for some other purpose, you must receive written permission from the donor.

CONTROL OF CONTRIBUTIONS

Whenever a not-for-profit organization accepts funds from the public, it assumes a stewardship responsibility to safeguard the contributed assets. This responsibility begins at the point where the organization *physically receives the gift.*

Funds collected in outside events or door-to-door solicitations should be managed by:

Maintaining records that show the names of individuals authorized to solicit on behalf of your organization. These records should indicate the amount of funds collected by each individual and the source of the funds.

Arranging for a deposit of contributions daily or weekly to avoid a large build-up of cash in the custody of anyone who is not bonded.

Funds received by mail may be controlled by:

Arranging for two people to open all mail and jointly prepare a list of amounts received.

Arranging for donors to send their contributions directly to your bank if it is not practical to have two volunteers open the mail together.

Similar controls should be established for special fund-raising events. Again, it is wise to employ the concepts of a) controlling the parameters of the potential giving by prenumbering and accounting for used and unused tickets, and b) limiting access by frequent deposit to significant amounts of unrecorded funds.

These may seem like somewhat unusual controls, but they do not need to be burdensome. You should be aware that these are the controls against which your organization can be held legally liable in case there is any dispute about your stewardship of funds solicited by your organization.

CONTRIBUTED SERVICES

Most local not-for-profit organizations in the international exchange field depend almost entirely on volunteers to carry out program functions. A question frequently asked is whether you can place a value on these contributed services and record them as contributions in your financial statements. The answer is a little complex.

In theory, there is no reason why such services cannot be recorded. They must, however, follow three basic rules: a) there must be reasonably good control over their use; b) there must be an objective basis upon which to value them; and c) you must be able to prove that the services are an essential part of your organization's activities.

The most difficult one of these three criteria to meet is valuation of contributed services. Unless your organization has a paid employee doing the same type of work, it is hard to calibrate. While this difficulty can be overcome by looking at comparable jobs, the paperwork involved in getting support for such work is many times more difficult than it's worth.

I would advise you to make some rough calculations of volunteer-time contributions for the purposes of fund-raising, but not to make these contributed services part of your official financial statement. It merely inflates your organization's budget and can distort the true size of your effort, since few other not-for-profit organizations officially include contributed services in their published financial statements.

Given the above vagaries of contributed services, I would certainly discourage you from encouraging people to see them as tax deductible. The recordkeeping this would subject you to would be more trouble than their service was worth.

ALLOWABLE VOLUNTEER DEDUCTIONS

For volunteers interested in some form of tax deduction from their work, there are some allowable deductions that you and your volunteers should be aware of.

First of all, any family hosting a teenage exchange student on an international exchange program may deduct fifty dollars a month for the student's support. This has been included in a special act of Congress. There has recently been discussion about trying to raise this to an amount closer to the current deduction for a dependent, but since this will take a Congressional amendment, it is likely that this will remain little more than a symbolic gesture of support for the hosting experience.

In any case, I would not suggest that any host family expect a financial offset for the experience. It will definitely cost money to host a student for a year. The payback will have to be seen in the nature of the experience and the relationship with the student—not in tax deductibility.

Other forms of deductions for volunteers are, however, more direct and commensurate. Volunteers may deduct phone calls, tools, parking, gasoline, and other out-of-pocket expenses associated with volunteering. In such cases, the best way to document this is to have an expense form which your treasurer can validate justifying the expense claimed. The volunteer then files this form as an in-kind contribution on her own tax return.

A final area where deductions are unquestionably appropriate is if you or any member of your chapter are selected to attend a regional, national, or international conference. The cost of all expenses associated with these is deductible. You should, however, be very careful of how you treat such trips if your spouse accompanies you. This makes the trip much more susceptible to IRS scrutiny, and justification of it as a deduction that much more difficult.

THE INDEPENDENT AUDIT

An audit is a series of procedures performed by an experienced professional accountant designed to test, on a *selective basis,* financial transactions and internal controls. The objective is to form an opinion as to the fairness of the way in which financial statements are presented for a given period. An audit is not an examination of *every* transaction that has been recorded.

In most cases, for a small, volunteer, not-for-profit community group, audits can be completed on a volunteer basis by a local accountant. For organizations operating on a cash basis, auditing tends to be relatively simple and should not require a great deal of time.

FEDERAL AND STATE REPORTING FORMS

You will not need to file a Federal Tax Return unless you have incorporated. If you have a tax-exempt status, you will definitely be required to file with the IRS. Once again, however, many local chapters of national exchange organizations are covered by their national organization's tax-exempt umbrella and reporting. If this is your case, however, you must be aware that the funds you work with on a local level really belong to the national organization from the day you receive them. You are therefore responsible to your national organization for reporting regularly on the use of your funds, so that it can report to the federal government in a consolidated statement of all its operations.

This latter point is one that many volunteers have difficulty understanding. It is, however, quite logical. Even though you raise money in your local community and spend it for local activities, if money is collected under a federal tax exemption, you must be accountable to the government for its usage. If you are not accountable directly, then you must be accountable to and through the organization that has given you your tax-deductibility in the first place. The only other option you have is to not allow tax deductions for financial contributions given you or to incorporate and obtain your own tax exempt status. Both seem to involve more problems than reporting to your national organization.

A number of states have laws requiring not-for-profit organizations to register with a regulatory agency prior to soliciting any funds within the state. This registration involves financial statements and sometimes an independent audit. In addition, there is an annual report. Most states exempt local unincorporated volunteer organizations from these requirements, but once again, they may hold your national organization liable for conducting business in the state. In such cases, the national organization will depend on you for reporting your finances so they can in turn fulfill your state requirements.

Here then are the "basics" of your group's finances—a budget, a checkbook to record income and source, expenditure and purpose, and a system of controls and reporting to ensure that you are maintaining stewardship over the money entrusted to you. This is budgeting, accounting, and controlling at the easiest and simplest level. If it gets any more complex than this, consult a local accountant (on a pro bono basis of course) to get advice on keeping it simple!

For Further Study

Bennett, Paul. *Up Your Accountability.* New York: Taft Corporation, 1973.

Bowe, Jr., Gerald G. *Where Do All the $ Go? What Every Board & Staff Member of a Non-Profit Organization Should Know About Accounting and Budgeting.* Concord, N.H.: The New Hampshire Charitable Fund, P.O. Box 1335, 1975.

Flanagan, Joan. *The Successful Volunteer Organization: Getting Started and Getting Results in Nonprofit, Charitable, Grass Roots and Community Groups.* Chicago: Contemporary Books, 1981.

Mason, Diane, Gayle Jensen and Carolyn Ryzewicz. *How to Grow a Parents Group.* Western Springs, Ill.: CDG Enterprises, 1979, Appendix B.

United Way of America. *Accounting and Financial Reporting—A Guide for United Ways and Not-for-Profit Human Service Organizations.* Alexandria, Va.: United Way Publications, 1974.

Program Evaluation and Volunteer Satisfaction

9

We have been concerned throughout this guide with two kinds of management: the management of international exchange programs and the management of the volunteers who work so hard to make them possible. In discussing the results of all the tasks and activities described thus far, we must consider both sides of the success equation—program success and volunteer satisfaction.

A program that has been successful at the cost of volunteer spirit and commitment is a short-term gain for a long-term disaster—it is simply unacceptable. One of the key aspects of volunteer-supported programs is that they have to meet the needs of the volunteers. Without this, your program will find itself in an irreversible decline. So, it is impossible to evaluate the results of your programs without considering their impact also on the people who made them possible.

PROGRAM EVALUATION: "HOW DID WE DO THIS YEAR?"

Evaluation of your local activities doesn't have to be complicated— remember that. Don't let me or anyone else intimidate you into thinking that you have to have some major study to determine whether you have been successful in your work. While a comprehensive study may be useful for your national organization, your local organization can gain a great deal from a more informal review of your programs and operations.

Try to approach program evaluation as the simple task of asking yourself "How did we do this year?" That's a question everyone asks from time to time and it's nowhere near as overwhelming as thinking about "program evaluation."

The most difficult part of program evaluation comes in your annual planning. At its simplest, evaluation starts with your statement of program plans in the beginning of the year and ends with the question— "Did we do what we said we wanted to do?" One observer of voluntary organizations formulated it this way:[1]

Planning. "If you don't know where you're going, you'll end up someplace else."

Evaluation. "If you don't know where you have been, can you really be sure you were there?"

In assessing the results of your work during the year, there are a few simple questions which you and your committee should ask yourselves.

DID YOU ACHIEVE YOUR GOALS?

This should be a simple enough question, but it may be difficult to answer if you have not gone through the goal-setting and planning process outlined in Chapter 3. It is very hard to talk about effective program evaluation as an afterthought. I know it's difficult to make yourself plan in a systematic fashion, but it takes only one meeting at the beginning of each year to outline your programs and objectives. If you take the time to do this, then the results discussed in this chapter will be a piece of cake!

WERE YOUR GOALS APPROPRIATE?

Remember your mission? At the beginning of this guide we talked about the mission of your group and the need to ensure that your programs continue to meet felt needs of the community, rather than just "doing what we did last year." The first question to ask yourself in evaluating your programs should therefore be—"Were our programs and goals appropriate; that is, did they meet felt needs in the community?" If turnout at an event was poor was it because the function you have held for the last ten years is no longer appropriate? If you are satisfied that you tried the right thing, then you can move on to the next series of questions to determine why you were successful or not successful.

WERE YOUR GOALS REALISTIC AND SPECIFIC?

One of the keys to determining why you were or were not successful in your program activities is to ask yourself whether your objectives were specific enough. Perhaps you felt during your planning process that you had been quite specific regarding your hopes and expectations, but now realize that you planned more programs and activities than you could carry out effectively. Without running the risk of quantifying everything to death, were you specific enough in your objectives to be able to assess in advance whether you had the resources to achieve them? This is often a problem encountered by people with fuzzy planning—they overreach because they have not thought things through in enough detail to realize in advance that they do not have adequate resources to achieve all their desires.

WERE YOUR ACTIONS WELL-TIMED AND COORDINATED?

A major problem encountered in many programs is poor timing or sequencing of activities. Too often things are put off until the last minute and then hastily arranged with inadequate resources. Another common problem is lack of coordination of tasks. Sometimes your "advance" publicity needed to bring people out to an event is in the paper the day of the event; or your program is planned for an international dinner, but no one has contacted the school to see whether their facilities can be used. In order to be sure that you are working in a well-timed and coordinated way, your monthly committee meetings should always look at least *three months* into the future and review how everyone's responsibilities are progressing for each activity. This way you will be sure that things do not fall between the cracks.

WERE YOUR RESOURCES ADEQUATE?

Needless to say, it is not a new phenomenon for people to bite off more than they can chew. It happens especially often in volunteer work. Well-intentioned people make commitments they sometimes don't fulfill, because 1) they can't say no when asked to do something, 2) they are committed to the purpose of the organization, but unrealistic about their own time availability or skills, 3) they enjoy the position or prestige of project leadership, but do not really know how to organize and lead people to get things done. Overcommitments and commitment for the wrong reason are the two basic reasons volunteers get into trouble. When assigning project responsibility, be careful about both these areas and question people privately if you are concerned about their ability to do the job they said they would do.

In addition to human resources, all programs take financial resources. If you ran into financial difficulties, was it 1) because you did not adequately anticipate costs in advance, 2) did not have controls on the project costs, resulting in a cost overrun due to poor management, 3) did not raise enough money to cover the project costs? Why did these things happen and what can you do to ensure that you operate more effectively next year?

That's all there is to it. Just ask yourself those questions at one of your year-end meetings and you will have done all the evaluation you need to do. Of course, you then need to ensure that the results of your evaluation are included in your next year's plan. If you are on an annual planning and review cycle, however, that is not hard—it happens automatically.

A final word: I truly believe that program planning and evaluation is not a difficult task in itself—the most difficult part is *scheduling the time to plan and review!* If you can promise yourself to set the time aside, the rest will come easily. So, do it now! Go get your calendar and write in it when you will meet with your group in the next year to review your last year's work and plan next year's. Go ahead—right now. Then you will have gotten over the most difficult part of the planning and evaluation process!

VOLUNTEER SATISFACTION: DID WE HAVE FUN AND A SENSE OF ACCOMPLISHMENT?

Another simple question—did you and the people working with you have fun and gain a sense of accomplishment from what you did last year? If so, why? If not, why not?

NEED SATISFACTION

You will remember from our discussion of volunteer needs in Chapter 5 that people join volunteer organizations for many reasons. Some work for the ideals of the organization and because they want to "help people." Others work because they need the affiliation with others. Some volunteer because they need the recognition and power that comes with volunteer leadership. Others are driven to help organizations achieve their objectives and are seeking a sense of service and accomplishment for themselves and their community.

When examining the satisfaction which you and members of your organization received from your work during the year, you and they should measure your feelings against some of these needs. One way to do this is to ask each person to state what he or she had hoped to get from their volunteer experience during the last year and what they feel they got. This is a good way to have a useful discussion, which many times can go into a review of the organization, its purposes, the way in which you work together, the roles and responsibilities people assumed or were assigned, and the way in which your group was seen in the community as a result of its activities. In the process, you will see the relationship between volunteer satisfaction and program success. For obviously the two are very much intertwined.

VOLUNTEER RECOGNITION

One of the greatest fallacies prevalent in volunteer organizations is to think that people feel they are giving themselves to a cause and do not need any rewards or recognition other than the satisfaction of a job well done. Everyone needs rewards of some kind, either extrinsic or intrinsic.

In Figure 13, we can see the results of data collected in a survey of volunteers conducted in early 1978. This reveals that many people are

Figure 13

Survey Results on Extrinsic and Intrinsic Volunteer Satisfaction

WHY DO PEOPLE VOLUNTEER?	% RESPONDING
Extrinsic Expectations	
—Training opportunities	66%
—Letters of appreciation	31%
—Praise from volunteer coordinator	31%
—Banquet	20%
—Pin	26%
Intrinsic Expectations	
—Opportunity to be of service to others less fortunate	90%
—Opportunity to do something interesting and unusual which adds variety to one's life	80%
—Opportunity for social interaction	77%
—Opportunity to get out of the house	49%
—Opportunity to be part of an important organization in the community	55%
—Opportunity to practice one's religious beliefs	45%
—Opportunity to fulfill an obligation to the community	63%
—Opportunity to test career possibilities	24%

Data excerpted from "Volunteer Work and Its Rewards" by Dr. Benjamin Gidron, *Volunteer Administration*, Vol. XI, No. 3, Fall 1978.

motivated by what are called "intrinsic" rewards—or the opportunity to receive satisfaction from the activity itself. In each of these cases, some personal need is being met.

In addition to intrinsic rewards, however, there is also recognition that can be given to volunteers outside of the fulfillment they feel from the activity itself. As is indicated, the opportunity for training has become a very popular expectation for many volunteers. Indeed, most of the organizations in the international exchange field have initiated regional training programs in recent years. One of the reasons for the popularity of training is that in most cases it provides insights and skills that are transferable to a range of life situations.

Opportunities for training are therefore a key factor in attracting and holding many volunteers today.

While training is the most popular extrinsic reward, there are others. To what extent have you provided adequate opportunities during the year or at the end of the year for people to say "thank you" to one another? This does not have to be a big dinner with the high school band and expensive wood and brass plaques (unless you want it to be!). It can just be wine and cheese after a committee meeting in which you celebrate someone's particular success or contribution to the work of your group. It can be during the year, after a project has ended well, or at the end of the year, after your evaluation meeting as a "thank you" to everyone who has worked so hard during the year.

Figure 14 lists 101 ways to give recognition to volunteers. There are many wonderful ideas here, both big and small. In some ways, the small ones are even more impressive, because they emphasize the "little things" we can do for one another.

In this regard, you should not forget personal recognition, in addition to public ones. Many times, it will mean more to a volunteer to get a hand-written note from you than to have all the parties and public words of appreciation that roll so liltingly off one's lips on such occasions. When I was president of AFS I had many opportunities to publicly thank volunteers and staff for work they had done. The most special moments, however, were when I sat down in the quiet of my office to write a longhand note to someone to thank them for something very special they had done. The feedback I received from these people was that the note had been a "very special" thank you for them.

Finally, we see in Figure 15 a summary of volunteer motivation, which has become a popular statement of volunteer expectations over the last decade. This statement is representative of the "new volunteer," who expects his or her time and energy to be well-used and wants to feel a sense of participation in planning the future of the organization. To satisfy this volunteer will take not only extrinsic rewards and recognition, but also a well-run organization that follows many of the practices and guidelines we have discussed. In the end, volunteer satisfaction and program success have the same source—a well-managed and well-led organization.

Program evaluation and volunteer recognition answer the questions "How did we do this year?" and "Did we have fun and a sense of accomplishment from our work?" These seem like obvious questions

Figure 14

101 Ways to Give Recognition to Volunteers

Continuously, but always inconclusively, the subject of recognition is discussed by directors and coordinators of volunteer programs. There is great agreement as to its importance but great diversity in its implementation.

Listed below are 101 possibilities gathered from a wide variety of volunteer organizations. The duplication at 1 and 101 is for emphasis.

It is important to remember that recognition is not so much something you do as it is something you are. It is a sensitivity to others as persons, not a strategy for discharging obligations.

1. Smile.
2. Put up a volunteer suggestion box.
3. Treat to a soda.
4. Reimburse assignment-related expenses.
5. Ask for a report.
6. Send a birthday card.
7. Arrange for discounts.
8. Give service stripes.
9. Maintain a coffee bar.
10. Plan annual ceremonial occasions.
11. Invite to staff meeting.
12. Recognize personal needs and problems.
13. Accommodate personal needs and problems.
14. Be pleasant.
15. Use in an emergency situation.
16. Provide a baby sitter.
17. Post honor roll in reception area.
18. Respect their wishes.
19. Give informal teas.
20. Keep challenging them.
21. Send a Thanksgiving Day card to the volunteer's family.
22. Provide a nursery.
23. Say "Good Morning."
24. Greet by name.
25. Provide good preservice training.
26. Help develop self-confidence.
27. Award plaques to sponsoring group.
28. Take time to explain fully.
29. Be verbal.
30. Motivate agency VIP's to converse with them.
31. Hold rap sessions.
32. Give additional responsibility.
33. Afford participation in team planning.
34. Respect sensitivities.

Figure 14 Continued

101 Ways to Give Recognition to Volunteers

35. Enable to grow on the job.
36. Enable to grow out of the job.
37. Send newsworthy information to the media.
38. Have wine- and cheese-tasting parties.
39. Ask client-patient to evaluate their work-service.
40. Say "Good Afternoon."
41. Honor their preferences.
42. Create pleasant surroundings.
43. Welcome staff to coffee breaks.
44. Enlist to train other volunteers.
45. Have a public reception.
46. Take time to talk.
47. Defend against hostile or negative staff.
48. Make good plans.
49. Commend to supervisory staff.
50. Send a valentine.
51. Make thorough pre-arrangements.
52. Persuade "personnel" to equate volunteer experience with work experience.
53. Admit to partnership with paid staff.
54. Recommend to prospective employer.
55. Provide scholarships to volunteer conferences or workshops
56. Offer advocacy roles.
57. Utilize as consultants.
58. Write them thank-you notes.
59. Invite participation in policy formulation.
60. Surprise with coffee and cake.
61. Celebrate outstanding projects and achievements.
62. Nominate for volunteer awards.
63. Have a "Presidents Day" for new presidents of sponsoring groups.
64. Carefully match volunteer with job.
65. Praise them to their friends.
66. Provide substantive in-service training.
67. Provide useful tools in good working condition.
68. Say "Good Night."
69. Plan staff and volunteer social events.
70. Be a real person.
71. Rent billboard space for public laudation.
72. Accept their individuality.
73. Provide opportunities for conferences and evaluation.
74. Identify age groups.

Figure 14 Continued

101 Ways to Give Recognition to Volunteers

75. Maintain meaningful file.
76. Send impromptu fun cards.
77. Plan occasional extravaganzas.
78. Instigate client-planned surprises.
79. Utilize purchased newspaper space.
80. Promote a "Volunteer-of-the-Month" program.
81. Send letter of appreciation to employer.
82. Plan a "Recognition Edition" of the agency newsletter.
83. Color code name tags to indicate particular achievements.
84. Send commendatory letter to prominent public figures.
85. Say "we missed you."
86. Praise the sponsoring group or club.
87. Promote staff smiles.
88. Facilitate personal maturation.
89. Distinguish between groups and individuals in the group.
90. Maintain safe working conditions.
91. Adequately orientate.
92. Award special citations for extraordinary achievements.
93. Fully indoctrinate regarding the agency.
94. Send Christmas cards.
95. Be familiar with the details of assignments.
96. Conduct community-wide, cooperative, interagency recognition events.
97. Plan a theater party.
98. Attend a sport event.
99. Have a picnic.
100. Say "Thank You."
101. Smile.

Vern Lake, Volunteer Services Consultant, Minnesota Department of Public Welfare.

to ask. They are, and people do ask them all the time. The trouble is that many volunteers ask them individually and never come together to ask them as a group. This year make sure you and your chapter conduct a review of your feelings about your work together. Ask the questions together—you'll find it a rewarding and useful experience. I guarantee it!

Figure 15

Volunteer Viewpoint

If you want my loyalty, interests, and best efforts, remember that . . .

1. I need a SENSE OF BELONGING, a feeling that I am honestly needed for my total self, not just for my hands, nor because I take orders well.
2. I need to have a sense of sharing in planning our objectives. My need will be satisfied only when I feel that my ideas have had a fair hearing.
3. I need to feel that the goals and objectives arrived at are within reach and that they make sense to me.
4. I need to feel that what I'm doing has real purpose or contributes to human welfare—that its value extends even beyond my personal gain, or hours.
5. I need to share in making the rules by which, together, we shall live and work toward our goals.
6. I need to know in some clear detail just what is expected of me—not only my detailed task but where I have opportunity to make personal and final decisions.
7. I need to have some responsibilities that challenge, that are within range of my abilities and interest, and that contribute toward reaching my assigned goal, and that cover all goals.
8. I need to see that progress is being made toward the goals we have set.
9. I need to be kept informed. What I'm not up on, I may be down on. (Keeping me informed is one way to give me status as an individual.)
10. I need to have confidence in my superiors—confidence based upon assurance of consistent fair treatment, or recognition when it is due, and trust that loyalty will bring increased security.

In brief, it really doesn't matter how much sense my part in this organization makes to you—I must feel that the whole deal makes sense to me.

I would add that I hope the whole deal makes sense to everyone involved—the client, staff, volunteer . . . and you.

For Further Study

O'Connell, Brian. *Effective Leadership of Voluntary Organizations.* New York: Walker and Company, 1981.

Wilson, Marlene. *The Effective Management of Volunteer Programs.* Boulder, Colorado: Volunteer Management Associates, 1976.

Part III:

MANAGING THE CROSS-CULTURAL EXPERIENCE: CULTURE SHOCK, COUNSELING, AND GLOBAL EDUCATION

Cultural Differences, Culture Shock, and Intercultural Adjustment

10

As we work in international exchange programs, all of us are affected by global political, social, and economic trends. We are challenged by people with differing beliefs to explain our own values under conditions that are in flux. We are confronted with the task of helping foreigners adjust to American situations and events that we ourselves do not fully understand. And we are faced with trying to understand what these changing values and beliefs will do to our own lives and the interdependence we have with many of the people with whom we are working in international endeavors.

These are significant and difficult tasks. But one of the most exciting and potentially important aspects of international volunteerism is that we are faced with the need to understand changes in our own and other countries. As a result, we have an opportunity to become more aware of the world in which we live and more atuned to evolving patterns that may increasingly affect all our lives.

It is important, therefore, for us to reflect for a moment on some of the broader social, political, and economic changes currently affecting the United States in order that we can better explain our society to those from abroad.

TEN CURRENT CULTURAL TRANSFORMATIONS IN AMERICAN SOCIETY

American society is currently searching for new meaning and focus after a period of convulsion in the 1960s and 1970s that left the country unsure of many of the basic precepts that have guided us from our beginnings. A new society is emerging with new needs and new priorities growing out of ten dramatic and still-evolving changes from the last two turbulent decades.

Some people may feel that these changes are behind us, but everywhere one looks their impact is being felt. Only time will tell how many may be reversed by a different political ideology. At present, they appear to be more social transformations than political or cultural trends; issues that reach beyond a particular political philosophy to the basic values of a people and their society.

These are the ten transformations as I have observed them:

1. *An equal opportunity transformation.* For minorities and women there is a new world, a new purpose, and a new future that paints a new landscape for the future of this country.

2. *A political authority transformation* in which post-Watergate, Vietnam suspicions, and monitoring of politicians and the political process have all but removed political heroes from the American scene.

3. *A family transformation* in which people have questioned marriage as the basis for social organization on an unprecedented scale that includes more frequent divorce and more open forms of cohabitation.

4. *A sexual transformation* through which new sexual mores have entered all phases of life, and liberation movements have challenged long-standing tenets of social and personal behavior.

5. *A participation transformation* through which workers, students, and citizens of all ages and levels are demanding

to be included in the decision-making that affects their lives at home, at school, in the workplace, and in all institutions in which they are involved.

6. *A drug transformation* in which people of all ages seek escape from increasing complexities and responsibilities through the use of drugs.

7. *A spiritual transformation* where people are asking questions of central purpose in ways that have moved from "God-is-dead" to the "Moral Majority" and have raised nontraditional "humanistic" issues of quality of life and work that are challenging the workplace and volunteer organizations.

8. *An information transformation* in which the amount of information, its storage, manipulation, analysis, presentation, and usage have become a new art form affecting the lives of everyone, requiring new skills and creating new challenges and dangers.

9. *An environmental transformation* which has placed limitations on growth, limitations on social and recreational life, and limitations on the present in recognition of the needs of the future, pushing time perspectives past where they have traditionally been and raising questions about what is of central importance.

10. *An international transformation* in which the traditional balance of powers and alliances are challenged, new political and economic forces emerge and fade at a more rapid rate than ever, terrorism is a new reality of unimaginable future dimensions, and the threat of nuclear proliferation and misuse remains a constant nightmare.

The implications of these changes for American volunteers and for work with foreign visitors is legion. Indeed, given the magnitude of the changes taking place, one might assume that we *all* may be in need of "culture shock counseling" as we attempt to deal with these new perspectives on life in American society and the world. While a systematic exploration of the ramifications of these changes is beyond the scope of this small volume, they provide a backdrop for us as we examine some of the cultural differences confronting foreign visitors to our society.

In the following section I have tried to sketch some of the ways in which American society differs from other societies in terms of our assumptions and values. This is not offered as a comprehensive overview, but merely a sampling of the kind of comparative analysis that anthropologists and sociologists are undertaking in order to gain a better understanding of the problems that arise in intercultural communication and international exchange.

CULTURAL ASSUMPTIONS AND VALUES AFFECTING INTERPERSONAL RELATIONS

All of us working with international visitors or foreign students will learn that people are different and that sometimes these differences cause misunderstandings. The often-quoted ideal that "if people could only get to know one another, they would be friends" is as dangerous as it is sentimental. Getting to know people is a necessary prelude to understanding and respect, but such knowledge alone will not resolve our differences nor ensure our liking people whose beliefs and ways are different from our own. The ability to deal constructively with differences that are sometimes threatening to us is one of the key skills of cultural adjustment, either across cultures or within our own culture.

As a local volunteer working with foreigners in your community, you face the same challenge that an American faces when he or she goes abroad—you must attempt to understand what it means to be a North American (in deference to our Latin American friends, we are talking here of North American values, even though at times we shall use the term "American" for shorthand purposes). Our effectiveness in working with international visitors many times will reside in our ability to diagnose their problems in a way that separates those caused by cultural differences from those originating in personality traits.

This is not an easy task, even for professionals. It is even more to ask from someone working as a volunteer. While it is a challenging experience, it is one that can be wonderfully rewarding when it is handled correctly. Not only do you have the satisfaction of helping someone successfully adjust to life in the United States, but you also have an opportunity to learn about the United States in the process.

In reviewing some of the basic cultural assumptions and values affecting interpersonal relations between North Americans and people from other countries, we need to understand that cultural misunderstandings start as differences in *perceptions*. In acquiring the assumptions and values comprising cultural attitudes, we all learn to categorize what we see in ways that make sense within our social, economic, and political milieu. As a result, there is perceptual diversity around the world (and even within this country) affecting the way people interpret life and the beliefs they have about the "right" and "wrong" ways of living and working together.

In order for us to step beyond questions of right and wrong, we must move to what Robert Hanvey calls "perspective consciousness."[1] This is an understanding that our perspective of the world is only one and that there are other ways of looking at things that are equally valid for others. This does not mean that we have to accept them as valid for ourselves, but we should allow others to hold their own beliefs, if these do not threaten our survival or peaceful coexistence.

To achieve perspective consciousness it is important for us to understand some of the fundamental dimensions on which cultures can be compared. Two of these are cultural assumptions and cultural values.

A *cultural assumption* is an abstract concept that unconsciously pervades a person's outlook or behavior. In other words, it represents an aspect of life that is seldom questioned, because the person has never known anything else and therefore "assumes" that this is the way the world operates. Typical North American assumptions are that everyone expects to be treated equally, enjoys assuming responsibility, and wants to participate in decisions affecting his or her future.

These assumptions are, of course, not true. There are many cultures in which "status" is more important than equality, because people are willing to trade off lower social status in return for economic security and well-being, as in the traditional *patron* system in Latin America. In such situations, people do not seek more responsibility and would not think of participating directly in decisions about their future made by people "wiser" than they who have taken on the obligation to care for them.

In each case, we are dealing with cultural assumptions, because people assume that everyone in the world lives the same way and they are unaware that any alternative would be acceptable. Obviously, one of the results of international exchange is that people can no longer hold on to their cultural assumptions as uneducated options. This does not mean that people have to change their beliefs, it only means that they must choose them in light of new options. When this happens, cultural assumptions turn into cultural values.

A *cultural value* is a predisposition that includes choice. People consciously choose to hold certain values as the result of examining options and determining that one value is better for them in their life than another. For example, in the United States, most people have decided that a democratic form of government with a free enterprise economic system is a better way to live than a socialist government with a centrally planned economy. These are values that are rationally selected, defended, and altered as the North Americans who hold them go through life. They are also the grist for differences of opinion about social, political, and religious issues that form the essence of the social and political dialogue of our society.

Cross-cultural misunderstandings in international exchanges arise from differences in both cultural assumptions and values. Assumptions are far more difficult to deal with, because they arise from a person's preconscious. In order to resolve problems on this level, the underlying idea must be brought to the level of consciousness so it can be recognized, identified, contrasted, and understood to be *one* perception of the world rather than *the* perception.

The list of cultural assumptions and values in Figure 16 includes some *dominant* cultural assumptions and values that Americans have and some prototypical values or assumptions that might be held by a person who comes from a society whose thinking is opposite from American society. When we speak of "dominant" cultural values or assumptions, we mean that they appear to be held by a *majority* of a society's population. This does not mean that everyone in the society is the same; it means merely that a majority of the people hold in common certain perceptions of themselves and their relationship to one another and the world.

Figure 16

Differences in Cultural Assumptions and Values Affecting Americans' Relations with Foreign Visitors

---

A   = Assumption or value held by majority of Americans

C–A = Assumption or value held by majority of persons of a "contrast-American society"; that is, one which is opposite of American society in its assumptions and values

I. How Do We See Ourselves?

    1. With whom do we identify?
        A: With ourselves as individuals
        C–A: As part of a family, clan, caste, or tribe

    2. What do we value in people?
        A: What people can achieve through their knowledge and skills
        C–A Who people are in terms of their educational or professional background, family heritage, or other affiliations

    3. To whom do we turn for help?
        A: Ourselves as independently resourceful people
        C–A: Our friends, family, and others owing us obligations

    4. How do we learn about life?
        A: From personal experience
        C–A: From the wisdom and knowledge of our elders

    5. How do we control our behavior?
        A: Through feelings of guilt because we are not living up to our personal standards
        C–A: Through feelings of shame because we are not living up to the standards of our family or community

II. How Do We See Our Relationships with Others?

    1. How do we relate to people of different status or authority?
        A: Minimize the difference; assume that everyone is equal
        C–A: Stress the difference; show deference for authority/position

    2. How do we greet one another?
        A: Stress informality; make people feel "part of the family"
        C–A: Stress formality; respect people's position and privacy

    3. How do we treat men and women's roles in society?
        A: Little differentiation between male and female roles
        C–A: Distinct and rigid differentiation between male and female roles

Figure 16 Continued

Differences in Cultural Assumptions and Values Affecting Americans' Relations with Foreign Visitors

4. How do we see male-female friendship?
   A: People may have close friends of both sexes
   C–A: People may have close friends of the same sex only

5. What are the characteristics of friendship?
   A: A loose concept applied to many people and based on overlapping special interests; limited obligations to one another
   C–A: A specific concept applied to a few people; total involvement based on mutual caring and respect; unlimited obligations to one another

6. How do we deal with conflict?
   A: Favor eye-to-eye confrontation between people disagreeing to resolve the differences
   C–A: Favor working through a third-party to manage disagreements without embarrassment of acknowledging their existence

7. How do we regard competitive kidding or joking?
   A: As acceptable, interesting, and fun
   C–A: As unacceptable and embarrassing

8. What are the primary means of social interactions with friends?
   A: Doing things together
   C–A: Being together

9. What is the preferred pace of life?
   A: Fast, busy with emphasis on getting things done
   C–A: Slow, steady with emphasis on getting the most out of life

III. How Do We See the World?

1. How does the world work?
   A: In scientifically observable and knowable ways
   C–A: In mystical and spiritual ways which are unknowable

2. How do natural forces operate in the world?
   A: In a rational, controllable manner
   C–A: In a predetermined, spiritually controlled manner

3. What is the role of fate in life?
   A: It has little influence; we are the masters of our destiny
   C–A: It has great influence; there is little we can do to alter it

Figure 16 Continued

Differences in Cultural Assumptions and Values
Affecting Americans' Relations with Foreign Visitors

4. What is the relationship between man and nature?
   A: Man can and should modify nature for his own needs
   C–A: Man should accept his environment and work within
        its limitations

5. What is our attitude toward things we desire in life?
   A: What is good or desired is unlimited if we work hard
        enough for it
   C–A: What is good or desired is limited and must be shared
        with others

6. How do we look at time?
   A: In precise minutes and hours by which we organize
        our days
   C–A: In diffuse days, weeks, or months by which we
        organize our years

7. How do we value time?
   A: As a limited resource not to be wasted
   C–A: As an unlimited resource to be used

8. How does life progress?
   A: In a lineal fashion through history
   C–A: In a cyclical fashion dominated by seasons and
        generations

9. How do we measure progress?
   A: In concrete, quantifiable units which indicate amount,
        size, percent that can be monitored and evaluated over
        time
   C–A: Against abstract social and moral principles which are
        immutable

10. On what basis are decisions made?
    A: Will it work?
    C–A: Is it right?

This guide is based upon a book by Edward C. Stewart entitled *American Cultural Patterns: A Cross-Cultural Perspective.* Washington, D.C.: Society for Intercultural Education, Training and Research, 1972.

HOW WE SEE OURSELVES

As Figure 16 indicates, there are many different ways in which we see ourselves. As Americans, we tend to see our primary identification as individuals, with strong emphasis on individual responsibility. We value people who can achieve competence and specialized skills, and we respect them as people with whom we would like to work.

With this emphasis on individuals and their expertise, we tend to believe that we can learn a great deal about life from our own personal experiences. As a result, we depend on people to control their actions by personal standards that are responsive not only to their own needs, but also to the general welfare of the community within which they reside.

There is, however, a contrasting view held by people from many societies. These people see themselves as part of a family, clan, caste, or tribe which is inseparable from their sense of self. Recognition of achievement for the individual is possible only as it is reflected in a sense of achievement for the group. As a result, people are concerned about background, family connections, and other affiliations. They depend a great deal on friends and family for assistance. In countries like Japan, for example, an elaborate network of obligations is established whereby people develop long-lasting patterns of assistance to one another as a result of past experiences.

This kind of culture has been described by Edward Hall, the well-known anthropologist, as a "hi-context" culture.[2] It is "hi-context," because people are seen within the "context" of networks that "define" who they are. In such cultures, it is important for people to know one another's backgrounds in much more intimate detail than in the more individualistic Western cultures. As a result, social rituals are more important, especially among strangers.

These rituals tend to last longer as people "size up" a guest in order to determine whether the person can be trusted.

Such intricacies are often not understood by Americans and other Westerners from "lo-context" individualistic cultures. Americans need only know the data necessary for working with a person within a specific task or project. We tend to evaluate people more on their "expertise" to perform certain functions than on their background and network of relationships.

When people from lo-context cultures meet people from hi-context cultures, the lo-context people are often impatient with the "how-is-your-family" routine, while the hi-context people are trying to gain information critical to their understanding of how to treat the other person. In such situations, lo-context people will rush into discussions with people from hi-context cultures that the latter consider premature. The result is that hi-context people feel rushed, and lo-context people classify them as "quiet, shy, or inscrutable."

Given these two views, it is easy to see how cross-cultural conflicts can develop as people come from group-oriented societies to a more individualistic American community. They may be reluctant to strike out on their own and take the kind of independent position that Americans many times interpret as a sign of expertise or competence. They also may seem reticent or shy as they are thrust into a situation where they no longer can depend upon their friends and family for assistance and guidance in approaching life situations.

In counseling persons from hi-context, group-oriented cultures (Japan being the "classic" case, but most of Asia, Africa, the Middle East, and Latin America also sharing some degree of this orientation), one must be sensitive to the need to take time to establish a relationship with a visitor before moving into personal questioning. While this may be a slow process, you can see its importance within the "context" of the differences just described.

HOW WE SEE OUR RELATIONSHIP WITH OTHERS

Social relationships constitute an arena where we often encounter the most difficulties in working with people from abroad. We can see from Figure 16 that there are a number of areas that can cause intercultural problems.

First of all, Americans have very specific preferences for equality in friendship and tend to stress informality in both social and work relationships. In social relationships, the recent women's movement is changing even further a relationship that was, by world standards, already equalized between males and females. At work, the women's movement has had a profound impact in establishing equal opportunity for women and others who have been discriminated against in the past.

At the same time, the American idea of "friendship" is a somewhat loose concept broadly applied to a range of people with whom one has an acquaintance. Many Americans have "friends" they play cards with, "friends" they go fishing with, "friends" they go to church with, and so on. In such cases, "friendship" is defined as "doing things with other people." I call this "functional friendship." It serves a specific function and many times is limited only to that function. Thus Americans can have many friends for many different purposes.

This phenomenon is not surprising given the fast pace of American life and the great mobility, both geographical and socioeconomic, of many Americans. Loyalties change, and need to change, easily. These may be loyalties to friends or organizations. This willingness to be mobile, to replace one set of friends in one part of the country with another set of friends who can serve the same functional purposes in another is part of the secret of American productivity and success. It takes a toll, however, on the kind of "friendship" with which much of the world is familiar. This is what I call "full friendship."

"Full friendship" is one that serves many purposes and is built over time. It is the kind that doesn't keep score of whose turn it is to provide the dinner invitation. It is the kind of friendship that can allow you to call someone at 3:00 A.M. to talk because you feel lonely or happy or confused. It is a friendship in which two people are one in spirit, caring, and commitment.

Full friendship, however, is not smothering—it is accepting. It is not possessive—it is freeing. It says "I believe in you and accept you, regardless of what you may think of yourself or the worst things you may have done." It is "I love to be with you when we can be in tune and I will let you go when you need to be alone, or with someone else, without being threatened by your need for something or someone else." That kind of friendship exists in the United States. But it is not as frequently encountered as in many other cultures in which there is less mobility and more interdependence among friends and relatives, both socially and economically.

It is interesting to note that the American preference for informality also is reinforced by the English language. English is one of the most informal languages in the world, simply because it has only one form of the second person singular in its verbs—that is, the "you" form. When one American addresses another, there is no need to differentiate between a formal "you" (*sie* in German, *vous* in French) and an informal "you" (*du* in German, *tu* in French). This has a great effect on the informal way in which Americans can deal with one another upon first meeting.

If you consider that many of the Asian tonal languages have four, six, ten or (with Vietnamese) even twelve different forms of the second person singular verb form, you can see where this would affect exchanges with strangers. In such hi-context cultures, one needs to know the age, status, background, and position of another person before one can choose which form of language to use in asking your first question after saying "hello"!

This informality in both language and style, as well as mobility in interpersonal relations, allows Americans to deal with interpersonal conflict in ways of much higher risk than is possible for people from other societies, in which relationships are stratified and long-term. By comparison, Americans have less to lose in confronting interpersonal conflict than people from more rigid social and professional structures. As a result, Americans like to "confront conflict" directly and "get things out on the table."

For many cultures this is unheard of—the risk is simply too high. As a result, people in these cultures use a third person to resolve conflicts. In this way, conflicts can be dealt with, but people can "save face" if differences cannot be worked out smoothly or to mutual satisfaction. Since there is never a direct acknowledgment by the two parties involved that there has been a dispute, the results of the dispute also do not have to be acknowledged! Instead, answers are concluded, but the relationship remains intact without loss of status or face on either person's part.

Americans' informality and prevailing sense of "every person for himself" is further expressed in the general pleasure we get from kidding or joking at the expense of others. "Oneupmanship" and competitive social interaction, while a favorite American pastime, can be the source of great problems for foreigners who are trying to discern the strange ways of the American people. In fact, this is not only true of social competition, but also true of the use of humor in general.

Humor is one of the most culturally bound forms of interpersonal behavior. Not only is it the most difficult level of linguistic accomplishment, but it is also the most dependent upon the cultural, political, and social context. As a result, "teasing" and "joking" with foreign visitors should be approached very cautiously. This is particularly difficult for people who tend to use humor as a means of opening new relationships.

As we can see from Figure 16, the profile of more formal, group-oriented societies establishes value orientations that contrast totally with the picture we have drawn of the dominant American view of interpersonal relations. In many societies, male and female roles are more differentiated both within and outside the family; men and women usually have close friends, but only of the same sex. Any relationship with a woman outside the family circle, especially in many Arab cultures, is considered to be *ipso facto* romantic, since the concept of close nonromantic friendships with the opposite sex just does not exist.

It is easy to see that a need for counseling can frequently arise from differences in these areas. Male-female relationships are a particular source of concern and anxiety. American films have portrayed the United States as unusually free sexually, and with the sexual revolution noted earlier, it certainly has become a more open society than many others around the world. The recent development of a liberated homosexual movement also introduces a new dimension, particularly into foreign student counseling. It is no longer just a question of male-female relations that need to be addressed in cross-cultural social counseling, but male-male and female-female as well.

On a lighter subject, the use of first names in the United States should be characterized as a national obsession. In fact, most Americans of equal age are insulted if you call them by their last name after an initial introduction! Obviously, this is not the case with many people from other parts of the world—including most Europeans—who are *much* more formal about the use of first names than Americans.

Finally, there are the nonverbal ways in which culture affects interpersonal relations. In some cultures, young people, as a sign of respect, have learned not to look an older person in the eye, but to gaze at the floor with eyes cast down. Such behavior, when you are trying to work out a problem between a young foreign student and an American host parent, will often be interpreted by the parent as a sign of insolence or indifference. From the young foreigner's perspective, however, this may be a sign of respect.

These are the kinds of cultural factors that will come into play as you seek to help international visitors adjust to their experience in your community. The problems may seem overwhelming at first, but after you have had some practice and can place them all in some context like the concepts outlined in this chapter, it becomes an intriguing, lifelong expedition to try to decipher and understand the depth and breadth of differences affecting our intercultural interaction!

HOW DO WE SEE THE WORLD?

Just as we have different ways of seeing ourselves and our relationship with others, we also have different ways of looking at the world around us.

In the United States, we Americans have spent two hundred years creating a nation. We have forged a forceful, dynamic lifestyle in which we change those things we feel need to be changed in order to move ahead in developing our country. In the process, we have often been too-little concerned about our environment and the natural resources we make use of. We have felt that nature was something that could be understood through scientific investigation and could be controlled as a result of these investigations. We have not believed that our lives were controlled by fate, but have tended to believe that we could be the masters of our own destiny. We have believed that we could modify nature for our needs—building tunnels through mountains and bridges over rivers and moving forests to create fields for planting. We have tended to believe that those things good for our lives, be they material possessions or friendships, were "unlimited" if only we were willing to work hard enough to acquire and maintain them.

In recent years, as we noted earlier, some of these cultural assumptions and values have been challenged. The quadrupling of oil prices by the OPEC countries in October, 1973, made many Americans realize that natural resources may not be as unlimited as they previously believed. In fact, some people are beginning to understand that the reason American supplies of natural resources have appeared "unlimited" is that we have been importing vast amounts of the world's "limited" resources into the United States for our consumption.

But natural resources are not the only areas for new world perspectives. Concern for the environment has grown as pollution gluts our cities. We have begun to see our capacity to move science faster than our social and emotional capacity to adjust to our discoveries. Areas such as biogenetics have raised the vision of a people who are able to do more scientifically than we are able to ethically determine how to use. And our spending for weapons of unimaginable self-destruction seems to increasingly outweigh our willingness to allocate resources to improve the quality of life that we are living.

All of these changes spell limitations. But the issue is to strike a balance. We have moved our society forward, because we have used scientific investigation to open new economic, social, and political frontiers. We have managed to deal with the social and political revolutions which have been unleashed by these steps forward (like the sexual revolution) in ways that have shown long-term prudence. We are forcing ourselves to be more conservationist in our consumption of natural resources while still improving our quality of life. If we can continue our slow process of taking potential revolutions and turning them into transformations, we will yet find ways to survive the enormous changes this society is absorbing.

In other areas, we are known internationally for our preoccupation with work and our measurement of time in hours and minutes, rather than months and years. We see time as a limited resource to be analyzed, scrutinized, allocated, subdivided, targeted, and above all *managed!* In the end, we have been pragmatists more than ideologues and our genius has been demonstrated in "rising to the occasion."

We will take any problem and assess needs, establish quantifiable goals, action plans, and dates by which we will feel accountable for its achievement or guilty for our failure to solve it. This drive toward achievement gives us an unending creativity to tackle new problems regardless of how unsolvable they may at first appear. It is likely that we will also apply this to the problem of limitations, finding ways to accept the limitations that nature is increasingly placing upon us on earth, as we begin to open space for new exploration and use.

But once again, we must realize that we have a rather unique way of looking at the world. There are others who see the world differently, with different value orientations and different cultural assumptions about what can and can't be done, what should and should not be done.

There are those for whom spiritual and transcendental values are more important than the quality of this life. While the recent Iranian experience may be an extreme example of spiritual dominance over all aspects of social, political, and economic life, it is not the only, nor the first. Ideologically oriented societies, most recently those which have been called communist, have long advocated the sacrifice of material welfare for higher socialist ideals.

For people driven by religious or political ideology, time takes on new perspectives. The past is more revered, because it is related to individuals who have set examples, rules, and aspirations. The present is less important than the future and the future is measured in generations, rather than in minutes, months, and production schedules.

But different time perspectives are not just true of religious or politically driven societies. There are many rural societies in which the integration of man and nature is more strongly felt—an existence which unfolds in a cyclical fashion through recurring seasonal and life patterns, because there is little change from one generation to the next.

As a result, progress is measured against abstract social and moral principles, which have evolved under the leadership of village and tribal elders. Social, economic, and political changes are viewed in terms of their effect on basic life rituals, and concern may be expressed about the degree to which proposed changes are compatible with the "natural" state of affairs believed to control life.

Since many of these cultural differences lie in the realm of unconscious assumptions rather than consciously held values, different world views are many times the most difficult areas in which to work cross-culturally. To make people aware of these differences may require a great deal of time and patience, but this awareness can be very important for all international visitors as they struggle to understand the meaning of American society, the motivation of the American people, and the relationship of America to the rest of the world.

Let us turn now to how you can help someone who is experiencing culture shock as a result of his or her confrontation with these vastly different cultural perspectives.

CULTURE SHOCK AND CULTURAL ADJUSTMENT

It should not be surprising that people who pass from one culture to another often experience a shock that temporarily destabilizes them and reduces their ability to function effectively.

Culture shock is a generalized state of disorientation often resulting in acute anxiety. From a medical perspective it is a "transient neurosis," or a temporary emotional disorder that reduces normal functioning.

The *symptoms* of culture shock can be any or all of the following:

- depression, lethargy, and fatigue

- irregular sleeping and eating patterns

- psychosomatic physical ailments

- generalized anxiety and discomfort

- fear for safety or excessive concern with hygiene

These symptoms may be minimal or severe, depending upon the degree to which the visitor has become disoriented by the new environment. In most instances, he may be unaware that he is suffering from culture shock. Instead, he is likely to attribute his problem to some particular aspect of the new culture or some relationship. At other times, the individual may be unaware that anything special is wrong, but just feel a sense of general malaise that reduces motivation for no apparent reason.

Once the symptoms of culture shock have been identified, they should be dealt with in a basic three-step process. These are causal diagnosis, reaction analysis, and intercultural-adjustment.

STEP 1: *CAUSAL DIAGNOSIS*

Culture shock is caused by the loss of the familiar aspects of one's normal environment and their replacement with things that are unfamiliar. Specifically, culture shock is caused by two types of phenomena—the loss of the familiar old environment and the simultaneous challenges of the new surroundings. Some of these phenomena are listed below:

Losses of the Old Environment

- loss of friends, family, and other human support groups

- loss of ability to communicate linguistically

- loss of understanding of what is expected in terms of appropriate social, professional, and personal behavior

- loss of capacity to perform at levels of excellence that have defined one's identity, for example, as an excellent student or as "the life of the party"

- loss of understanding of the meanings of nonverbal communications

Challenges of the New Environment

- new sensory experiences—sounds, smells, sights

- new pace of life and patterns of behavior

- new role or position that does not match previous experience or self-concept

- new personal relationships that create problems

- new performance demands that exceed previous experience; for example, a higher level of willingness to take risks in experimenting with new behavior

It is important to help a person experiencing culture shock to identify as *specifically as possible* potential causes from the list above. Just the process of tying generalized anxiety or lethargy to some specific causes can help people feel more in control and able to deal with their situation.

STEP 2: *REACTION ANALYSIS*

The second step in assisting a visitor to deal with culture shock is to help in finding a reaction pattern to their experience. There are three typical ways people react to new cultural situations. These are flight, fight, and adaptation.

Flight

When a person responds to a new situation through *flight,* he or she rejects those people and things that cause discomfort and increasingly withdraws from opportunities to interact with them. This normally results in placing "blame" on the local people for being stupid, primitive, or unsupportive. In some cases, the individual places blame on her or himself for the inability to respond effectively to the new situation. Whichever is the case, the result is an increasing desire to isolate oneself from interaction that is threatening or perceived to be challenging and unsupportive.

One of the most common means of retreat is to spend more and more amounts of time with people in similar situations, most often with other foreigners. Foreigners can become a crutch to one another in ways that prevent successful adjustment to the local culture. They not only provide much-needed support, but also in most cases will readily re-enforce one another's belief that most of their difficulties are the result of the "natives' " inabilities and unsophisticated ways of behaving.

A second form of retreat, however, which is less often identified as a maladaptive behavior, is when a foreigner "goes native" in a new culture. This involves totally denying one's past and trying to identify completely with the norms, values, and beliefs of the host country. This is a maladaptive response, because it does not allow for the healthy integration of one's past with the present. The latter is a necessary process for establishing an integrated self-concept that can endure over time and is developed as a result of confrontation and reconciliation, rather than denial.

Developing a state of *dependence* on a new culture by fleeing from one's own culture is therefore just as dangerous as fleeing from the new culture. While "going native" may be temporarily satisfying, the ultimate effects of denying one's own cultural identity may be more harmful than beneficial.

Fight

Other people respond to a new culture with hostility and aggression. They become aggravated with those around them for making them feel ill at ease and as a result become determined to "show the natives how to do it the right way." Such visitors *fight* the new environment, trying to change the culture to which they have come. This state of *counterdependence* usually results in the foreigner's being isolated by the host culture or, in some cases, actually resisted to the point that the visitor does not accomplish many of the objectives of his stay.

People who respond to new, different situations with impatience and hostility toward others need to be made aware of what they are doing and how they are many times chasing after the proverbial windmills of Don Quixote. In most instances, their reactions are merely displacing or transferring frustration from one situation to another. These defensive reactions result in a great deal of misdirected energy, which is at the least inefficiently and most often inappropriately applied.

Finally, hostile, impatient behavior in most cultures is poorly received. In hi-context societies, it will result in the visitor never having an opportunity to become known in a way that allows him to achieve his objectives. If personal integrity and interpersonal sensitivity are highly valued characteristics in many cultures of the world, hostile, impatient behavior is one of the fastest ways to end the openness of one's hosts.

Adaptation

Finally, there are those people who start the slow and painstaking process of cultural *adaptation* and adjustment. In such an approach, the visitor does not reject his own culture or the new culture, but tries to understand his own feelings and anxieties, analyze their potential causes, and determine ways to approach the new culture from a "win-win" context.

In essence, the objective is to become *interdependent* with the new culture and its people. Interdependence assumes two equally independent forces coming together to complement strengths and weaknesses in a way that meets both needs. To do this requires a knowledge of self and others, which is crucial to successful adjustment.

STEP 3: *INTERCULTURAL ADJUSTMENT*

Once the symptoms, causes, and reactions to culture shock are understood, the visitor will be ready to understand that there is a longer-term cycle to successful adjustment. This is represented in Figure 17 and explained on the next several pages.

While there has not been any definitive empirical research supporting the stages of this cycle, many people involved in international exchanges report that it is very descriptive of the process experienced during their sojourn abroad.

If you are involved in a program that hosts people on a short-term basis, it is also important to recognize the dynamics of this process, because experience has shown that stages 1–4 often occur even during a three- or four-week stay and are even more prominent during an eight- to ten-week summer exchange experience.

Interestingly, the human psyche seems to adjust itself to the time available. In most cases, a visitor will experience a dip in Stage 3 about one-third of the way through, whether this is the second week

Figure 17

Intercultural Adjustment Cycle

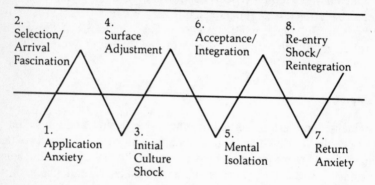

1. *Application Anxiety.* When waiting for an opportunity to go abroad, people experience anxiety over their chance of selection and their ability to handle their new opportunity. During this time, many anticipate cultural differences but have only a superficial awareness of potential adjustment problems.

2. *Selection/Arrival Fascination.* When a visitor hears that he or she will be going abroad, the person experiences a rush of elation. This excitement continues (with some small exception just before departure, when anxiety flares momentarily) until some time after the individual arrives in the foreign country. During this stage, expectations for the visit are high and the predeparture proceedings, as well as the arrival introductions, provide new stimuli and excitement about the potential of the new opportunity.

On arrival, the visitor tends to be the focus of attention and activity. He or she may be shown a level of respect and concern seldom—if ever—experienced at home. This reinforces one's self-concept and contributes to a general feeling of satisfaction and success.

3. *Initial Culture Shock.* The initial fascination, along with the rounds of introductions and parties, soon fades for a visitor who is remaining in a community over a period of time. Even for visitors coming to the United States on tour, the novelty of the foreign culture wears off after a few weeks and most people experience a decline in spirit known as initial culture shock. Characteristics of this period include possible changes in sleeping habits, excessive fatigue from speaking and listening to a foreign language, a lack of motivation to get up in the morning, general disorientation and uneasiness, and possible hostility toward some particular people or aspects of the society.

4. *Surface Adjustment.* After this initial "down," which usually does not last more than a few days to a few weeks, a surface accommodation takes

Figure 17 Continued

Intercultural Adjustment Cycle

place between the visitor and his environment which allows him to function at a relatively normal level without excellence. His language improves to the point where he can communicate basic ideas and feelings without fatigue and he learns how to navigate within a small group of friends and associates.

5. *Mental Isolation.* At some point, however, there is a desire for a deeper experience, greater language proficiency, and the return to excellence in performance which the visitor many times experienced back home. At this point the intractability of learning a new language proficiently is encountered, as are the inherent and often chronic weaknesses of the experience itself. This may be in the form of a misplaced professional or living situation, or an unfulfilled major objective of the visit. Unresolved conflicts with friends, hosts, or peers can also contribute to a sense of isolation.

6. *Acceptance/Integration.* At some point the visitor makes the important turnaround out of his mental isolation and decides to change those things which can be changed and make the best of the rest. When he is finally at ease with his profession, school, or interests, as well as with language, he is able to examine more carefully the new society in which he is living. Deeper differences between him and others become understandable and he finds ways of dealing with them. He may complain of the lack of true friendships as he experienced back home, but he has come to recognize that these kinds of relationships are hard to build in a year in a society prone to more "functional friendships."

Eventually, as he comes to accept himself and the situation in which he is living, he becomes more integrated into his surroundings. This transition, however, depends much more on his own attitude and willingness to "come to terms" with his experience than it is dependent upon someone coming to his rescue or discovering any dramatic change in the nature of his stay. Once the visitor has come to terms with himself in the new situation, as well as his expectations versus the potential of the reality, then he can relax and feel at home in his new surroundings.

7. *Return Anxiety.* Once settled in, the thought of leaving the new and familiar friends, faces, and community raises new anxieties similar to those experienced during Stage 1, before his departure. He begins to sense how much he has changed and how much his new community has become the comfortable home for his new personality. The thought of returning to his old life and the possibility of being challenged to go back to his old ways is threatening and anxiety producing. He fears that the people back home will not understand him and his new feelings and awareness. He may even feel guilty for wanting to stay and not return home, because he knows that there are many people anxiously awaiting his arrival.

Figure 17 Continued

Intercultural Adjustment Cycle

This is a time of great confusion and considerable pain. If the visitor has come from a great distance there is the fear that the friendships formed may never be experienced again. Especially for young people, oceans divide individuals not just by miles but by time, because the expense of transportation can mean waiting years before they can be reunited. This can be a period of great pain. But the greater the pain, the deeper was the experience, and, over time, the more lasting may be the benefits.

8. *Reentry Shock/Reintegration.* Upon returning home there are a number of shocks. There is the "role shock" as one is no longer "special." The visitor is not only not treated in a special way, but in many cases deep changes are not recognized and acknowledged. People claim to be interested in hearing about his trip, but whenever he starts to tell them in depth what it meant to him, they are unable to relate to it and many times drift away. No one seems to understand the nature of the experience, nor care about its existential impact.

There is also the confusion of returning home to people he has shared an entire life with, with whom he may no longer be comfortable. He may have changed in such fundamental ways that he can no longer gain emotional support from his relations at home and he is simultaneously grieving over the loss of friends in his foreign community. The combination can be devastating in the short-run and in many ways even more difficult than the initial shock when first abroad. The depth of the disillusionment comes from the fact that he had expected fulfillment and the feeling that there is no longer anywhere to go to feel "at home."

Final resolution of this stage of adjustment involves an integration of the overseas experience and culture, with one's new self-concept and with the realities of the back-home situation. This is a major life transition which, when successfully maneuvered, produces a new level of maturity and insight into oneself and the world. Once this is achieved, he will be able to turn to ways in which to become an active contributing force in his "new" old life.

---

of a six-week experience or the fourth month of a one-year experience. The extent, depth, and length of these dips will depend on the amount of support the visitor receives and the degree to which the symptoms, causes, and reactions can be successfully identified and understood.

Even if you are entertaining someone for only a few days, you may find that he or she has been away from home for two or three months and is perhaps in one of the low stages of the adjustment cycle. If this happens, you should be aware that it is a normal phenomenon and that you can sometimes assist by merely explaining the idea of such a cycle. It might even be helpful to show the visitor the diagram in Figure 17 and discuss some of the symptoms and causes of culture shock noted above.

It is useful for every international visitor to have an understanding of the intercultural adjustment cycle. Experience has shown that one of the most distressing aspects of culture shock is that people feel somehow they have "failed" and that their situation is unique and different from everyone else's. Some people may hide culture maladjustment better than others, but most people experience some disorientation.

It is important, therefore, for people to be made aware that these feelings are in most cases "natural" reactions to their situation, that there is a cycle to these feelings and that with a little bit of thought, analysis, and planning, they can get turned around and adjusted to the new cultural context.

In the next chapter we shall consider some specific techniques for working with foreign students who may be in your community on a longer term basis and may need more structured counseling assistance. Keeping in mind the cultural assumptions and values we just discussed, and the components of culture shock and the stages of the adjustment cycle, you should be gaining an overview of some of the factors that make cross-cultural counseling a uniquely challenging and rewarding experience.

For Further Study

Brown, Ina C. *Understanding Other Cultures.* Englewood Cliffs, N.J.: Prentice-Hall, 1963.

Hall, Edward T. *Beyond Culture.* Garden City, N.Y.: Doubleday, 1976.

_____. *The Hidden Dimension.* Garden City, N.Y.: Doubleday, 1966.

_____. *The Silent Language.* Garden City, N.Y.: Doubleday, 1959.

Hanvey, Robert G. *An Attainable Global Perspective.* New York: Global Perspectives in Education, 1975.

Harris, Philip R. and Robert T. Moran. "Managing Cultural Shock," *Managing Cultural Differences.* Houston, Texas: Gulf Publishing Company, 1979, pp. 82–100.

Lanier, Alison R. *Living in the U.S.A.* Chicago, Ill.: Intercultural Press, 1981.

Rhinesmith, Stephen H. "Americans in the Global Learning Process," *Annals of the American Academy of Political and Social Science,* No. 442, March 1979, pp. 98–108.

————. "Training for Cross-cultural Operations," *Training and Development Journal,* March 1970, pp. 20–23.

Stewart, Edward C. *American Cultural Patterns: A Cross-Cultural Perspective.* Washington, D.C.: Society for Intercultural Education, Training and Research, 1972.

Tornbiorn, Ingemar. "Culture Shock and the U-Shaped Adjustment Curve" in *Living Abroad: Personal Adjustment and Personal Policy in Overseas Setting.* New York: John Wiley & Sons, 1982, pp. 90–118.

Wedge, Bryant M. *Foreign Visitors to the United States and How They See Us.* Princeton, N.J.: Van Nostrand, 1965.

Cross-Cultural Communications and Counseling

11

Given the range of cultural factors examined in the last chapter, normal American counseling practices should be approached with a certain amount of sensitivity to their application to foreign students on international exchange programs.

It is important at the outset to stress that I am not trying to make you a professional counselor in a few pages of this book. I assume that the people with whom you will be working are for the most part emotionally balanced and reasonably well-adjusted individuals who are experiencing a temporary rather than chronic period of emotional instability. Most foreign students merely need someone to listen to them and help them understand their feelings as they try to adjust to a new living and cultural context.

If you do find yourself in a situation where you are called upon for on-going counseling, you should immediately contact someone at the national headquarters of the organization sponsoring your student to obtain advice concerning how you can turn the situation over to a professional counselor.

Assuming, however, that there may be times when you need to help your visitor "think through" his experience, let's examine some counseling concepts and practices that may be useful for you.

THREE COUNSELING SKILLS

Effective counselors do basically two kinds of work. They *facilitate problem management* by helping others resolve crises, deal with concerns, overcome difficulties, manage problem situations, and improve their psychological well-being.

They also *facilitate growth and development* by helping people discover their potential, develop their resources, and increase their ability to make decisions.

Counselors accomplish these two objectives—problem-solving and personal growth—by doing three things:

1. PROVIDING SUPPORT FOR THE PERSON

They are considerate, they listen, respond with understanding, and are available for help. They fulfill the first part of the old psychological dictum: "Be soft on the person, hard on the problem."

2. PROVIDING CHALLENGE

Just as challenge without support can be harsh, support without challenge can go nowhere. Ideally, counselors help people challenge themselves to gain new insights and understanding into their feelings and behavior and change those aspects getting in the way of a full, meaningful life.

3. PROVIDING A FRAMEWORK FOR ACTION

The best counselors are accomplishment-oriented. They are not there to "hold clients' hands," but to help them manage their lives more effectively. Since there is work to be done, they provide the structure enabling people to mobilize their resources more effectively in the management of problem situations. They help people see how to solve problems without taking the problems on as their own.

THREE MAJOR STAGES IN THE COUNSELING PROCESS

Gerard Egan, a well-known counseling professor at Loyola University, has developed a three-stage problem-solving model that provides a framework within which the counseling process can be viewed.[1]

These three stages are outlined in Figure 18 below. They involve the development of a present scenario, a preferred scenario, and an action program.

As we shall see, each of these stages in turn is divided into three steps. These steps are also indicated in the pie chart in Figure 18.

STAGE I: PRESENT SCENARIO: PROBLEM/OPPORTUNITY IDENTIFICATION

In this stage, you work with your student to describe and clarify the difficulty, concern, crisis, or problem situation he or she is facing. This involves three basic steps:

STEP 1. *IDENTIFY THE PROBLEM/OPPORTUNITY*

Help the person describe the situation as specifically as possible.

STEP 2. *FOCUS AND CLARIFY WHAT'S WRONG*

Help the individual disentangle the problem, explore it, clarify it, and focus on some central part of it that will provide leverage for managing the rest of it. This is the time to use the ideas about cultural differences, culture shock, and the intercultural adjustment cycle we discussed in the last chapter. Try to help the visitor sort out whether any of these factors may be creating problems. In these first two tasks, discovering and appreciating the person's perspective is crucial.

STEP 3. *DEVELOP NEW PERSPECTIVES*

Again using the checklists, challenge blind spots that the person doesn't seem to be seeing. Examine new ways of looking at issues and try to determine new sources of insight into how the problem came about, why it has become an issue right now, and what parts of it might be most easily addressed with some good chance of success.

STAGE II: DEVELOPMENT OF A PREFERRED SCENARIO

In this stage you help the person draw up a scenario that is preferable to the current situation. Ask him or her to describe what

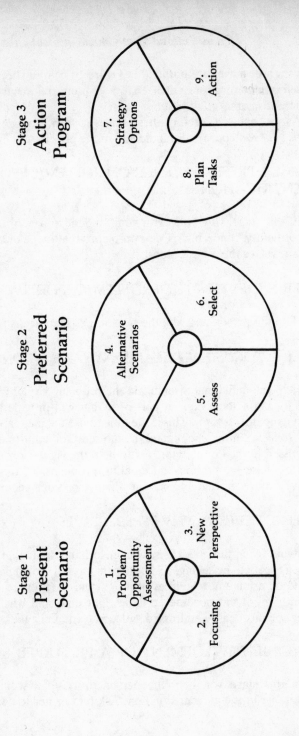

Figure 18

Three-stage Problem-Solving Process

Stage 1
Present
Scenario

1. Problem/ Opportunity Assessment
2. Focusing
3. New Perspective

Stage 2
Preferred
Scenario

4. Alternative Scenarios
5. Assess
6. Select

Stage 3
Action
Program

7. Strategy Options
8. Plan Tasks
9. Action

the situation would look like if the problem were solved. Be sure to test whether the solution would solve the current difficulty or whether it would merely affect a tangential but not decisive aspect of the problem.

STEP 4. *DEVELOP ALTERNATIVE SCENARIOS*

Help your student brainstorm a number of scenarios that would solve the problem. Try to develop at least three as a way of ensuring that all creative possibilities have been tested.

STEP 5. *ASSESS THE ALTERNATIVES*

Work with your student to assess each alternative, examining the advantages and disadvantages of each not only with regard to desired outcome, but also with regard to ease or difficulty of its achievement.

STEP 6. *SELECT ONE PREFERRED SCENARIO*

Based upon the results of the assessment, select one scenario that appears to be the most promising and use this as the basis for the next stage.

STAGE III: ACTION PLANNING

During this final stage, help your visitor review and test strategies for realizing the preferred scenario. This involves systematic planning with specification of tasks, assignment of responsibility, and determination of a timetable by which certain actions will take place.

STEP 7. *IDENTIFY GENERAL STRATEGY*

Examine whether the solution lies within your student, in another individual, in a relationship, or in the environment. Determine who or what needs to be changed in order for the preferred scenario to be achieved.

STEP 8. *DEVELOP SPECIFIC TASKS*

Determine specific tasks that need to be implemented. Examine sequencing, establish target dates when possible, and determine who will be responsible for each step.

STEP 9. *MONITOR ACTION*

Determine in advance how your student will review progress on the situation and the means by which the student will assess whether or not the chosen strategy is succeeding.

This is a model that has proven extremely effective in counseling a wide range of people about a variety of problems. You will note that it is very similar to the planning model we discussed in Chapter 3. This is because both are based on a model of individual and organizational change which are the same. In the end, changing organizations is the same as changing and managing the individuals within those organizations!

CULTURAL INFLUENCES ON THE COUNSELING PROCESS

The model we have just outlined is a standard American counseling process. While the general theory and stages can be applied to almost any culture, the process itself often needs to be adjusted for cultural differences. Just as the problems your visitor faces may be subject to differing cultural interpretations, so the process of counseling is also affected by differences in cultural assumptions and values.

The following chart lists some of the cultural assumptions and values that underlie most U.S. counseling theory and training, contrasted with assumptions and values that might prevail elsewhere, and are most probably represented by visitors from other countries with whom you will be working.[2]

AMERICAN VS. OTHER CULTURAL ASSUMPTIONS AND VALUES

American Assumption/Value	Contrast-American Assumption/Value
1. People (clients, counselors, and everyone else) are isolable individuals	1. People are integrally related to other people in groups such as families
2. Personal growth and change are valuable and desirable	2. Conforming to time-tested ways of behaving is desirable
3. Individuals have control over their own life circumstances	3. One's life circumstances are dictated by external forces (political, economic, social, or natural)
4. Personal problems are often soluble, through greater understanding of their origins and/or through remedial action undertaken by the individual	4. Problems are fated to occur and fate may or may not remove them
5. "Professional" people can help other people solve their problems a) people (counselors) can be genuinely interested in the welfare of strangers b) people (counselors) can be dealt with as occupants of roles	5. One's problems are beyond the control of other human beings a) only one's close friends and relatives can be trusted b) other people are dealt with as whole people
6. Open discussion of one's problems can be beneficial	6. It can be dangerous to reveal oneself to others
7. Emotional disturbances have their root in the individual's past	7. Emotional disturbances have their root in external forces or situations
8. People are (more or less) equal	8. There is a hierarchical ranking of people in society
9. Males and females are (more or less) equal	9. Males are superior

These fundamental differences in cultural assumptions and values reflect many of the differences touched on in the last chapter. While you will probably not encounter many of these differences as a major problem in dealing with Europeans, they are very much part of the Asian and African belief systems and to a lesser extent are shared by Middle Easterners and Latin Americans.

CROSS-CULTURAL COMMUNICATION PATTERNS AND THE COUNSELING PROCESS

Finally, the counseling process can also be affected by differences in communications patterns. John C. Condon and Fathi Yousef, in their excellent book, *An Introduction to Intercultural Communication*[3] describe some communication patterns which as North Americans we should be attentive to in dealing with people from other cultures.

1. THE USE OF SILENCE

In general, North Americans are much more uncomfortable with silence than people from many other cultures. Silence is many times a form of communication. It says, "I feel comfortable enough with you that I don't feel that I have to talk" or "I need to think about what I am feeling for a minute and I appreciate your just being next to me without talking." The next time you are with an international visitor, be aware of the degree to which you "need" to talk versus the amount you "would like" to talk in order to feel comfortable.

2. LANGUAGE SKILLS

Speaking a foreign language requires many skills: memorization, pronunciation, conceptual patterns of equivalence, and many other aspects that are difficult to learn to coordinate. You may very well find a visitor who has difficulty expressing himself and being understood. When this happens, the guidelines in Figure 19 may prove useful. The best advice is to take your time and speak s-l-o-w-l-y.

Figure 19

Guidelines for Counseling Across Language Barriers

When counseling someone cross-culturally, you should be aware that difficulties with English will often be a barrier to expressing and understanding true feelings. It is important to remember that no matter how intelligent a person is, he or she may feel stupid or cut off when struggling to understand what is being said to express thoughts clearly in a foreign language.

Here are a number of ways of dealing with language difficulties in the counseling process:

Speak slowly and simply

This doesn't mean speaking *louder* (which is a common mistake), it just means slowing down, enunciating your words carefully, trying to avoid the use of slang and advanced vocabulary.

Watch your counselee's face

See if some comprehension registers that can be nonverbally recognized. If you ask "Do you understand?" the response will many times be yes when the reality is no.

Repeat the thoughts until you are sure the other person has understood

Occasionally, ask the person to repeat back to you what you said to test level of comprehension.

Face the individual when you speak

Try to reinforce your words nonverbally with facial expressions. Facing the person will also help them in understanding your enunciation.

Do not worry about the correctness of English usage

A counseling session should not be an English lesson! In fact, overattention to English grammar and pronunciation may actually discourage the visitor from speaking.

Figure 19 Continued

Guidelines for Counseling Across Language Barriers

Encourage your visitor to also speak slowly

Heavy accents are hard to understand. It is perfectly acceptable for you to ask your counselee to speak slowly in order for you to understand better, just as you are speaking more slowly for the same reason.

Listen carefully to what is being said and try to avoid interrupting or completing sentences

When someone is having difficulty expressing themselves, it is natural oftentimes to try to help them complete their thoughts. This should be done very selectively to ensure that you are not replacing their thoughts with your own.

Use nonverbal gestures

While nonverbal communications are sometimes difficult to interpret cross-culturally, there are many basic nonverbal gestures which can be used well to not only reinforce verbal communications but occasionally to replace them.

Praise for genuine success

When the counselee makes a true breakthrough in thinking or understanding, show your enthusiasm with their success. Everyone needs positive feedback!

Be patient

In the end, counseling someone from another culture, just like adjusting to another culture, is often a slow, painstaking process. You must remind yourself to be patient. In the end your common sense, imagination, and respect for the visitor's needs will be your greatest assets in helping overcoming any problems.

*If you concentrate on these techniques, you will find it surprisingly easy to talk with visitors, even those who have the most severe language difficulties.

---

3. NONVERBAL COMMUNICATION

This includes the physical gestures accompanying our linguistic communication, which reinforce points we are making or deny what we are saying verbally. Nonverbal communication is probably the most important and least understood form of communication across cultures. Researchers are just beginning to try to categorize non-verbal communication differences for specific cultures, but a great deal of work remains to be done. Until there is more work in the area, the following list will provide an idea of the kinds of things you can explore with your international visitors in attempting to gain a better grasp of their behavior and helping them to understand yours:

hand gestures

facial expressions, such as smiles, frowns, yawns

posture and stance

clothing and hairstyles

walking behavior

interpersonal distance

touching

eye contact and direction of gaze

smells

speech rate, pitch, inflections, and volume

color symbolism

taste

cosmetics

time for arrivals and departures

It has been estimated that only about 30 percent of what is communicated in a conversation is verbal.[4] This is based upon two persons of the same culture speaking the same language. Given the cross-cultural situations we face in international exchange programs, we are probably even more dependent upon nonverbal communication. This means that something over 70 percent of our communications will be nonverbal!

SOME CAVEATS

In light of all the cultural factors we have examined which can affect cross-cultural communications and counseling, a few caveats are necessary as you experiment with the three-stage counseling model we have outlined in this chapter.

DO ONLY WHAT IS NECESSARY

Not all these nine steps in the model form part of every counseling situation or relationship. Sometimes you may only need to do one of them and the visitor may be able to do the rest.

DETERMINE WHICH STEP OF THE MODEL IS YOUR BEST ENTRY POINT

Once you listen to the visitor's problem, you need to examine which of the nine steps would be the best starting point. The visitor may have already defined the problem well, but not be able to formulate an action plan.

DON'T EXPECT THE MODEL TO PROCEED IN A STEP–BY–STEP FASHION

It is possible to jump around in the model. For example, the visitor might select a strategy, but determine through the action-planning process that it was not the best strategy. Be prepared to go to whatever part of the model seems best. To determine your strategy, sometimes it's better to share the model with the person you're working with so that you can together determine where to concentrate your energies.

ADAPT THE MODEL TO CULTURAL VARIATION AND SENSITIVITIES

As we have more than adequately detailed, cultural differences will be part of every aspect of your counseling process. Rather than letting this intimidate you, use the concepts, checklists, and ideas in this chapter to help you as you work with your visitor to untangle the real reason for an adjustment problem. I guarantee you, you will learn an enormous amount about yourself, American culture, and your visitor's culture in the process.

DO NOT ASSUME UNNECESSARY RESPONSIBILITY

Remember that the best solution will be one that the visitor identifies with and accepts responsibility for. In some cases, he or she will be more than willing to "give the problems to you," depending on you to solve it through intervention with others. Try to avoid taking on unnecessary responsibility, unless you are absolutely forced to by cultural differences. This doesn't mean that you should refuse to help, but be sure you are not trying to "rush in to fix things," as Carl Rogers would say.

DEAL WITH YOUR OWN FEELINGS AND NEEDS AS WELL AS WITH THOSE OF THE VISITOR

Be sure you are not responding to your own need for power or your own need to be liked. Figure 20 provides a series of self-evaluation questions you may find useful in ensuring that you are counseling from the right motives.

DESPITE ALL THE MODELS AND GUIDELINES PRESENTED IN THIS CHAPTER AND THE LAST, DO NOT BE OVERLY CONCERNED WITH ASKING THE "RIGHT" QUESTION OR USING THE "RIGHT" STEP IN THE COUNSELING PROCESS

The best counselors are the most natural ones—the people who feel comfortable in a counseling situation and who are there because they want to be, not because they feel they have to be. If a foreign visitor in your community needs counseling, accept the task only if you feel you would sincerely like to help. If you don't like the person, or doubt your ability to handle the situation, pass the job on to someone else who you think can do better.

Figure 20

Counselor Self-Evaluation

Here is a series of questions which you may want to ask yourself in evaluating your performance as a counselor of foreign visitors in your community:

Am I able to hear what is being said and implied about the counselee's feelings and attitudes without prejudging the results?

Am I able to listen so as to try to understand the thinking, motivation, and biases of the counselee in describing her situation and working out any difficulties?

Am I able to put myself in her place and see her situation from her point of view?

Do I understand that not only do I have the right to influence others, but they also have the right to influence me?

Do I know my prejudices and cultural assumptions and values, so that I do not block out messages that are unfamiliar to me?

Do I understand that people send messages in nonverbal ways and that I must "hear" this kind of communication too?

Do I understand that when a person feels she is being understood, she tends to be more open?

Do I understand that being a good listener does not mean I must agree with what the speaker is saying?

Do I understand that I am learning little about the other person and her perspective when I am talking?

Do I try not to overreact to emotionally charged words?

When I disagree with something, do I make a special attempt to listen carefully?

If I am having trouble being understood, do I understand that the burden is on me to try to understand the other person?

Do I consider the needs of the person, as well as the situation?

Do I listen for what is *not* being said?

Do I look as if I am listening and interested?

Do I listen for feelings behind the words, as well as the words?

Do I know when I may be intimidating my listener by threatening behavior?

If I were the counselee, would I want to be counseled by me?

SOME FINAL REMINDERS

The chief thing to remember is that the best way to approach a counseling session is to feel as natural and relaxed as possible. Armed with the information in this chapter and the one before, and a belief in your own ability to sit down and relate to another person, you can make the counseling process an interesting and challenging opportunity to use your intellectual and interpersonal skills.

Counseling should be something you do because you enjoy it and feel some confidence that you can be useful to others. Don't force yourself to become involved in counseling if you feel that you are not the right person to be a counselor.

In any case, as we noted at the beginning of this chapter, you should never become involved in a long-term counseling process. In fact, if your counseling of a foreign visitor goes on for more than three or four sessions, you should probably consider the possibility of referral to some professional person in your community. Obviously, for a short-term visitor of a few days or few weeks, this is not a problem.

However, if you have a foreign student in your community for six months or a year, you may become more intensely involved and feel at some point that a transfer of relationship is necessary. It is important that you be aware of this possibility and that you know when to step out. No one creates more problems than a counselor who stays with a relationship longer than he or she should, thereby preventing the counselee from gaining the independence necessary to continue his life in the community.

Counseling can be a deeply stimulating, rewarding, insightful process, not only for those whom you are helping, but also for you. I hope with some of the ideas outlined in this chapter and the one preceding, you will receive even greater satisfaction from your encounters with foreign visitors in the future.

For Further Study

Brislin, Richard W., Stephen Bochner and Walter J. Lonner (eds.). *Cross-cultural Perspectives on Learning.* New York: John Wiley & Sons, 1975.

Condon, John C. and Fathi Yousef. *An Introduction to Intercultural Communication.* Indianapolis, Ind.: Bobbs-Merrill, 1975.

Egan, Gerard and Michael A. Cowan. *People in Systems: A Model for Development in the Human-Service Professions and Education.* Monterey, California: Brooks/Cole Publishing Company, 1979.

Egan, Gerard. *The Skilled Helper: Model, Skills and Methods for Effective Helping.* 2nd edition. Monterey, California: Brooks/Cole Publishing Company, 1982.

Hall, Edward T. *Beyond Culture*. Garden City, N.Y.: Doubleday & Company, Inc., 1976.

_____. *The Hidden Dimension*. Garden City, N.Y.: Doubleday & Company, Inc., 1966.

_____. *The Silent Language*. Garden City, N.Y.: Doubleday & Company, Inc., 1959.

Horner, David and Kay Vandersluis. "Cross-cultural Counseling" in *Learning Across Cultures*. Washington, D.C.: National Association of Foreign Student Affairs, 1981, pp. 30–50.

Morain, Genella G. *Kinesics and Cross-Cultural Understanding*. Washington, D.C.: Center for Applied Linguistics, 1978.

Morris, Desmond, J. Collett, F. March and S. O'Shaughanessy. *Gestures*. Yarmouth, Maine: Intercultural Press, 1978.

Pedersen, Paul, J. G. Draguns, W. J. Lonner and J. Trimble (eds.). rev. ed. *Counseling Across Cultures*. Honolulu: University Press of Hawaii, 1981.

Exchange Visitors as Global Educators

12

In the two previous chapters we have seen how you can assist your foreign visitors to better understand their experience in the United States and adjust to the differences they find here. But there is another side to managing the cross-cultural experience. This is the opportunity you provide for your community to be exposed to the foreign visitors your organization is sponsoring. As we shall see in this chapter, this exposure is especially needed in our schools, where we must educate the leaders of tomorrow about the international world in which they will be living.

While one of the benefits of international exchanges has always been the informal interaction between visitors and people in a community, many local exchange program leaders today are developing new ideas about how to ensure that their visitors are exposed to a greater number of community people in a more systematic manner.

THE NEED

There are basically two reasons for this increased interest in more formalized exposure.

First, community exchange leaders are faced with the very pragmatic need to raise greater and greater amounts of money to support their exchange activities. As they search for new sources of income, it becomes increasingly necessary to show the benefits that their exchanges bring to populations broader than just the visitor and his or her host family and friends.

Second, American educators have become more and more concerned that there is a dearth of international understanding among many elementary- and secondary-school-aged children today. Recent studies have indicated shocking statistics about the level of international awareness and "global literacy" (as it has come to be called) of American high school students. Consider for a moment the following facts:

- One study in 1974 of a national sample of how much school children know about other nations and other peoples revealed that over 40 percent of the twelfth graders could not locate Egypt correctly, while the same number were persuaded that Israel was an Arab nation.

- When asked, one out of every five of these high school seniors was unable to pinpoint the whereabouts of France or China.

- A UNESCO education study of 30,000 ten- and fourteen-year-olds in nine countries placed American students next to last in their comprehension of foreign cultures, but first in their knowledge of local, state, and national affairs.[1]

This "global illiteracy" exists in a country which is at the center of international economic, political, and military affairs. Consider these facts:

- The crops from one out of every three acres harvested in the United States are exported. More than half our wheat, soybeans, and rice are sold abroad.

- The United States is either completely or almost totally dependent upon imports for such key minerals as platinum, diamonds, manganese, tin, bauxite, nickel, chromium, and cobalt.

- Nearly half the profits of the top 500 corporations in the United States result from foreign investments and sales, and one American in six owes his or her employment to foreign trade.[2]

Further, in a society with a democratic form of government, the citizenry needs an even more sophisticated understanding of international matters, because the policies of the government are subject to popular review and consent through the electoral and legislative process. Without an informed citizenry, it is impossible for a democracy to have an informed foreign policy. Without an informed foreign policy, it is impossible for a country of the power and importance of the United States to expect to live in peace and prosperity well into the 21st century.

The young people in our elementary and secondary schools today will be responsible for national leadership from the years 2015 to 2040. Yet most are being inadequately prepared by their basic educational experience to deal with the basic life issue with which they will be faced—living internationally.

The educational imperative for broader international exposure has become so evident that a sister "movement" to the international exchange program has recently emerged. It is called "Global Perspectives in Education." This is comprised of a network of educators throughout the United States who are working together with local, state, and national school officials to find ways to formally introduce more global awareness into the kindergarten through twelfth grade curriculum. A list of some of the organizations in this area can be found in Appendix I.

While the global-perspectives movement faces many obstacles from lack of teacher awareness and skills to inadequate curriculum materials and attitudinal barriers, a surprising amount of progress has been made in some communities and states around the United States. Many excellent publications and audiovisual presentations are available that provide information about other countries, cultures, and cross-cultural communication. But there is also an extremely valuable, largely untapped, resource in many U.S. communities that could be utilized to bring a more global perspective to U.S. schools—the international visitors of programs like the one you lead.

YOUR COMMUNITY EXCHANGE ORGANIZATION AS A GLOBAL EDUCATIONAL RESOURCE

Did you ever think of part of the mission of your organization as helping your local school system "internationalize" its perspective? While I am sure that this may have been one of those unconscious objectives behind your exchange activity, I would like you to think for a minute about the possibility of making this a much more explicit part of your committee's mission.

Your organization is probably the perfect place for a speaker's bureau on global awareness or international affairs. Think of the outreach you could have in your community if you were to work with local school teachers and officials to provide resource people and materials in international studies to augment local classes in your elementary and secondary schools. Not only would you be providing a service that is badly needed in most communities, but you would also be introducing many new people to your organization and its work!

I am sure that you have probably already worked to coordinate the activities of your high school exchange students (foreigners and American returnees) as speakers in your school. If you were to create a position like Speaking Coordinator for Global Perspectives, you could offer your services to a wide range of groups in your community beyond the school and in the process make them aware of your exchange activities. In fact, there are many sources for speakers beyond the students who may be in your local program.

SOURCES FOR SPEAKERS ON GLOBAL PERSPECTIVES

If you look around in your community, you will find a vast array of people with international experience. Consider the following:

FOREIGN STUDENTS AT UNIVERSITIES IN YOUR AREA

While the number of foreign students participating in officially sponsored (AFS, Youth for Understanding, etc.) high school exchanges in the United States is only a little more than 10,000 per year, there were 336,985 foreign students at U.S. institutions of higher education in the academic year 1982-83. This is a vast resource of talent that could be available for your local school, but *someone must organize it.* Your international exchange organization is as good a place to start as any!

OTHER SHORT–TERM FOREIGN VISITORS

Many local councils for international exchange are responsible for arranging programs in their communities for foreign visitors who are traveling around the United States learning about the American people. What better way to acquaint them with an American community than to enable them to meet and speak with a class of students at a local elementary or secondary school? With adequate preparation, the class can be ready to ask questions about the visitor's country and engage in an exchange which can be delightful and educational for everyone involved.

Local Sister Cities and Friendship Force Committees are excellent avenues for bringing short-term visitors to your local school children. These organizations many times bring large groups of people from another community to stay in an American counterpart community for a brief period of time. In such group exchanges, there is a "critical mass" of people which allows for a diversity of activities in your local school, including a "national day," assemblies, and an international dinner. If the group is large enough, it can move throughout the school system in such a way that almost all the children can have a simultaneous exposure to another country and its people.

INTERNSHIP PROGRAMS

Organizations like AIESEC (the International Association of Students in Economics and Business Management), the Association for International Practical Training, and 4-H bring young people to the United States for internship experiences in business, industry and agriculture. These people have no formal relationship with a school system, even though they may be here for extended periods of time. They also provide a resource that could be used in local schools: people who are living and working with Americans and have a unique perspective on American society and who can speak on a range of issues.

LOCAL BUSINESSMEN AND WOMEN WHO TRAVEL INTERNATIONALLY

If you are willing to expand beyond those persons officially involved in exchange activities, you will find that almost every community today includes some people who travel internationally on business. These people often have a vast amount of experience and broad perspectives on the world, which they could usefully share with young people in your schools. The problem is that no one has asked them. No one has taken the time to coordinate their interests with the needs of your school teachers. To do this could be an enormously rewarding brokering experience for your organization, and in the meantime you would probably recruit a few more host families and supporters!

OTHER LOCAL PEOPLE WITH INTERNATIONAL EXPERIENCE

There are many other people—those who have traveled extensively for pleasure, returned Peace Corps volunteers, retirees who traveled worldwide during their working years—and others who are also potential resources. Many would be flattered and delighted to be asked to help in the education of the young people in your community. They merely need the opportunity.

So—there is the pool of talent available for you. You can either limit your activities to coordinating the exchange visitors' program or you can extend it to others in the community, depending upon your group's mission, goals, and resources. Remember, however, that expansion to include local businessmen and other resources in your community means an extra opportunity for you to receive publicity, recruit new members, and raise funds from people who learn about your organization and become interested in supporting it.

Now, assuming that you were interested in this expansion of your work as means for additional service, publicity, membership recruitment, and fund-raising, what exactly would you be asking these people to do?

OPPORTUNITIES FOR "GLOBAL EDUCATORS" TO CONTRIBUTE TO YOUR COMMUNITY

There are some excellent activities in public schools throughout the United States that use foreign students, local foreign residents, and Americans who have studied abroad. The kinds of projects and programs that have evolved in recent years include:[3]

CLASSROOM ACTIVITIES

Foreign visitors and returned American travelers can share information and impressions about other countries and comparisons with life in the United States. When possible such visits should include some basic introduction to the speaker's language, no matter how difficult it may be. Experience has shown that young people are fascinated by linguistic differences in this kind of introductory encounter.

When working with elementary school children in particular, visits are more beneficial if they can occur on at least three different occasions.[4] In this way, young people and the international visitor begin to feel at home with one another, and the inherent "strangeness" begins to disappear. Activities can be conducted in all subject areas, not just the most obvious ones of social studies and foreign language. Physical education classes could include a unit on games or dances from other countries; home economics could prepare food from other countries; music classes could study music from abroad, and so on with art, literature, and other subjects.

INTERNATIONAL FAIRS AND SPECIAL NATIONALITY CELEBRATIONS

These can be arranged for the entire community. This is particularly good when you have a visiting group such as the Friendship Force Committees or Sister Cities might sponsor. In such fairs the foreigners share food, crafts, music, customs, and other aspects of their home countries.

LOCAL SPEAKING OPPORTUNITIES

Foreign visitors can speak to local business and civic clubs about life in their country and make observations about their visit to the United States. It is important to note that foreign high school exchange students are encouraged not to speak publicly about their visit before the January of their school year. This allows them to become adjusted to their new life, assimilate some of the differences in cultural values and assumptions, develop their English language skills, and become secure enough to make presentations in a foreign environment. If you need speakers for a fall meeting, therefore, you should look for other resources in universities or short-term visitors.

LANGUAGE BANKS

Foreign students in particular can serve as language resources for people in hospitals, nursing homes, tourist centers, shopping centers, police stations, etc., when people in these situations need interpreting assistance.

These examples all focus on activities that can *enhance* the current school curriculum, not replace current subjects with new courses on "international affairs." This is important. With many special interests clamoring to have their particular needs met in today's public school curriculum, it is important to note that the "global perspectives" movement is merely attempting to add an international dimension to subjects *already being taught.* There is plenty of room in the curriculum for different perspectives on current subject matter—that is the beauty of this effort and one of the reasons it dovetails so well with international exchange organizations.

In Appendix II we have included descriptions of six model global education experiences selected by the National Association for Foreign Student Affairs as exemplary activities utilizing foreign exchange students as global educational resources. You may want to refer to these for further ideas.

BENEFITS OF USING FOREIGN VISITORS AS GLOBAL EDUCATORS

Recent research has provided some new insights as to why it is particularly useful to use exchange visitors, and, in particular, exchange students, as educational resources in local schools.[5]

These findings indicate that "awareness and appreciation of host country and culture," "foreign language appreciation and ability," "understanding other cultures," and "international awareness" are areas in which high school exchange students show the most growth as a result of their exposure abroad. These studies also show that exchange students are superior to nontraveled students in their ability to communicate facts and feelings to others. (The latter, however, may well be a function of selection more than a result of the experience itself.)

As can be seen in Figure 21, the AFS Impact Study, which was conducted over five years and is reported in four reports written between 1981 and 1983, revealed that "awareness and appreciation of host country and culture" was the area that showed the greatest average increase from pretest to posttest. This was defined as "considerable knowledge of the people and culture of my host country and an understanding of that country's role in world affairs." AFS students increased an average of 15.4 points from pre- to posttest on a 100-point scale.

But sometimes passing on this knowledge-gained faces considerable obstacles. In a second study conducted with YFU students after their return to the United States from a summer in Japan, the students were asked to list examples of what they considered silly questions and stereotypic comments made to them by Americans. Analysis of the questionnaires led to the development of four categories of questions and comments: confusion between Chinese and Japanese, broad neutral questions, stereotypical questions, and anti-Japanese comments. The students' reactions clustered around telling the facts, speaking positively, using humor, feeling angry and/or frustrated, and recognizing cultural relativism.

More than 92 percent of the students indicated that the best way to combat ignorance was by "telling the facts." This included one student's response to statements such as "all Japanese are short" by explaining that she had a Japanese neighbor six feet tall. In another case, a

Figure 21

Personal Growth from an Intercultural Homestay

Chart comparing changes of AFS students with changes of nontraveled students.

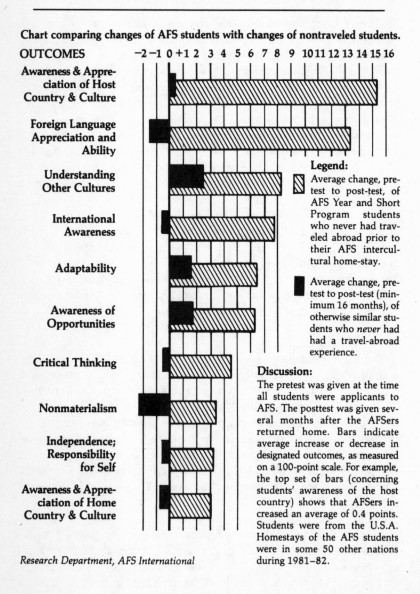

OUTCOMES −2 −1 0 +1 2 3 4 5 6 7 8 9 10 11 12 13 14 15 16

Awareness & Appreciation of Host Country & Culture

Foreign Language Appreciation and Ability

Understanding Other Cultures

International Awareness

Adaptability

Awareness of Opportunities

Critical Thinking

Nonmaterialism

Independence; Responsibility for Self

Awareness & Appreciation of Home Country & Culture

Legend:
Average change, pretest to post-test, of AFS Year and Short Program students who never had traveled abroad prior to their AFS intercultural home-stay.

Average change, pretest to post-test (minimum 16 months), of otherwise similar students who *never* had had a travel-abroad experience.

Discussion:
The pretest was given at the time all students were applicants to AFS. The posttest was given several months after the AFSers returned home. Bars indicate average increase or decrease in designated outcomes, as measured on a 100-point scale. For example, the top set of bars (concerning students' awareness of the host country) shows that AFSers increased an average of 0.4 points. Students were from the U.S.A. Homestays of the AFS students were in some 50 other nations during 1981–82.

Research Department, AFS International

Figure 21 Continued

Personal Growth from an Intercultural Homestay

Research Identifies Benefits for Youth of Intercultural Homestays Abroad

The chart on the first page illustrates the principal finding of a major study completed by researchers based at AFS International/Intercultural Programs, Inc., in New York. This Impact Study employed a rigorous research design and involved nearly 2500 secondary school students from the U.S. and many other countries.

The basic question addressed by the research project was this: Do secondary school students who have an intercultural homestay abroad develop and mature in positive ways more rapidly than similar students who have no such experience?

The research team began by talking at length with newly returned AFS students; team members discussed with some seventy students in Europe, Latin America, and the U.S. how their values, knowledge, awareness, skills, and other personal characteristics had been changed by their intercultural experience. These students' statements were confirmed by eight hundred additional newly returned AFSers from around the world who were contacted by mail. Using this information gathered from young former AFS participants, the research team identified seventeen personal characteristics, or "outcomes," that were widely believed to improve markedly as a direct result of an intercultural homestay in another country.

A questionnaire employing a sophisticated self-rating technique was then developed to measure these seventeen characteristics. After pilot-testing, the questionnaire was sent in January 1981 to thousands of students who had applied to participate in the Year and Short Programs offered by AFS. Most of these applicants subsequently went on an AFS exchange experience. Others, however, did not participate for a variety of reasons; these nonparticipants formed a "comparison group." About four months after the AFS students returned home, they were asked to complete the same questionnaire a second time. The students in the comparison group also were asked at this time to complete the questionnaire again.

By giving the same questionnaire to these two groups of students at two different times—before and after some of them had participated in an AFS program—the researchers were able to measure the amount of change that had occurred in each of the seventeen characteristics, and to compare the average changes of the AFS students with those of the students in the comparison group. The researchers discovered, with respect to ten of the characteristics, that the AFS students experienced a significantly greater amount of positive change than that of the students

Figure 21 Continued

Personal Growth from an Intercultural Homestay

---

who had not had an AFS experience. This is the principal finding of the Impact Study.

This finding is illustrated by the chart. The hatched bars indicate the average change of the AFSers; the solid bars show the average change— sometimes negative—of the students in the comparison group. The bars depict the average increase or decrease in the designated outcomes (personal characteristics) as measured on a 100-point scale. Note that the bars do not indicate percentages. (The differences between the average scores of the AFS students and the comparison group on the other seven outcomes were negligible.)

This research finding is unambiguous evidence that an intercultural homestay abroad enables secondary school students to learn and grow to an extent well beyond what could be expected due to normal maturation. In short, an intercultural homestay accelerates the personal growth and development of young people.

Many other findings resulted from the AFS research project. Some are of interest primarily to social scientists; others lend support to the principal finding reported on this sheet. Complete accounts of the methods and findings of the Impact Study will appear in appropriate professional journals during 1984 and 1985. For more information, write to the Research Department, AFS International, 313 East 43rd Street, New York, NY 10017, U.S.A., or telephone 212-949-4242 extension 302 or 303.

---

student was asked "Did you just eat rice and raw fish?" to which he answered "Yes, rice was part of most meals. Sometimes we ate sushi, but there are many other kinds of Japanese food which are delicious. Occasionally we ate at McDonalds, Pizza Hut, or Arbys!"

It is good sometimes to have someone who has been there help explain what life in another country is like.

The YFU study revealed that students had a better sense of what it was to be an American and how that contrasted with another culture. For example, when asked "Do they wear normal clothes?" a student answered: "They wear a lot of the same clothes Americans wear. Sometimes especially older people wear Japanese kimonos, but mostly just for festivals. Our clothes are not right or correct or normal. You were just raised differently and not knowing any other way makes you think you're normal. What if you were born in Japan or elsewhere?"[6]

About 14 percent of the YFU students said they could recognize cultural relativism before they went abroad and 80 percent said they used such a response frequently after their return. The ability to respond nondefensively, in an objective manner that shows the differences existing between countries, is not easy and cannot be expected from all international visitors or Americans who have traveled abroad. The research shows, however, that there is a greater likelihood of a school class getting a culturally relativistic picture of another culture from someone who has been there than from someone who has not.

OBSTACLES TO USING EXCHANGE VISITORS AS GLOBAL EDUCATORS

While all of this seems quite straightforward, there are some real problems in trying to coordinate international resources with the timing and need of teachers and the potential insecurity some may feel due to their own lack of international experience.

There are four typical problems which are encountered:

1. "WE STUDIED GERMANY LAST MONTH; SORRY YOU DIDN'T CONTACT ME SOONER."

Timing is a real problem, not just an excuse from people who don't want to be bothered. To overcome this, you should have your global speaker resource coordinator send a questionnaire out at the beginning of the school year to all teachers and other people in the community who might be interested in an international speaker, asking when during the program year they might like an international resource for the class. Then you can plan the year, with adequate time to identify resources to meet needs that are known in advance. As in everything else, a little advance planning can help a lot.

2. "HOW CAN THEY TEACH US WHEN THEY AIN'T TALKING GOOD ENGLISH LIKE US DO?"[7]

This is one way of explaining the language problem! Teachers and students are often embarrassed if they cannot understand someone with a heavy accent or poor grammar. If you have resource people

who have some language difficulty, it is best if you or someone from
your local organization who can understand them accompanies them
to the classroom and "co-teaches" the class in a way that allows you to
act as an interpreter/facilitator when language barriers loom in the
way.

3. "PEOPLE WHO HAVE BEEN ABROAD ARE BRAINWASHED AND AGAINST THE UNITED STATES."

Many Americans are rightfully proud of our country and are
sensitive to what they feel may be criticism or somewhat unfavorable
comparison of the United States with other countries. In fact, one of
the questions most often asked of educators in the global education
movement is "Can you be supportive of international education and
still be patriotic to the United States?" John I. Goodlad, the eminent
dean of the Graduate School of Education of the University of
California at Los Angeles, reported in his recent book, *A Place Called
School*, that there is little " . . . inclusion of global or international
content. Over half of all the students in our sample believed that
foreign countries and their ideas are dangerous to the American
government."[8]

Such reactions obviously take patient responses from those of us
who have traveled internationally and believe in the importance of an
informed global perspective. Again, it is a good idea for someone
from your local committee to brief a visitor from abroad about local
sensitivities prior to any speaking engagement and, if possible, to
accompany the person so as to be able to help if there are any
problems of interpretation that arise.

4. "I DON'T HAVE TIME FOR A LOT OF INTERNATIONAL DISCUSSIONS, I HAVE TOO MUCH TO COVER ALREADY TRYING TO DEAL WITH ALL THE STATE REQUIREMENTS THAT HAVE BEEN PUT ON ME FOR MY SUBJECT."

There is no question that the fight for time in the classroom,
especially at the secondary level, is a real one. The problem of
introducing global perspectives into a classroom is, however, not
really a curriculum or a time problem. In the end, it is instead a

matter of awareness and commitment on the part of the teachers. A recent national survey revealed that only 2 percent of all teachers have taken a course dealing with any aspect of international affairs. It is therefore not surprising that many are not adequately enough committed to want to make room in their classrooms for international speakers. In such cases, it is best to try to work with these teachers and assure them that you or someone else from your organization will be present to help utilize the resource person. You can also see whether there are activities outside the classroom that could help students gain a better perspective on other countries.

A NEW COMMITMENT

In the end, these and other objections can be overcome if you are clear about how you would like to manage your exchange visitors as resources for your local schools, church, and civic associations, and for other interested individuals and organizations in the community.

The best way to make this happen is to include it in your planning process, which was discussed in Chapter 3. This will take a conscious commitment. It means allocating human and financial resources and planning in advance how your students or visitors will be made available as resources to your local groups. In many cases, as we have noted, you may have to start by educating your community about the potential benefits to be derived from having a foreign visitor speak to them. This becomes the first step in broadening your outreach as an international exchange organization.

Your commitment to manage the cross-cultural experience of your visitor is a considerable undertaking. If you and your group are willing to expand your mission in this way, however, you can discover some wonderful new opportunities for service to your community and the world!

Further Study

Cross-cultural Learning in K-12 Schools: Foreign Students as Resources, The National Association for Foreign Student Affairs, 1860 19th Street, N.W., Washington, D.C., 20009

Hoopes, David S. (ed.). *Global Guide to International Education.* New York: Facts on File, 1984.

Improving International Understanding: A School District Planning Guide, Indiana/ Kentucky International Understanding Project, New Albany-Floyd County Consolidated School Corporation, 802 E. Market Street, New Albany, Indiana, 47150

Intercom: A Curriculum Journal for Teachers and Students. Global Perspectives in Education, 218 East 18th Street, New York, New York, 10003. GPE is also the coordinator of most of the global education movement in the United States and is an excellent resource center.

Internationalizing Your School: A Handbook for Teachers, Administrators, Parents and School Board Members, by Frank Rosengren, Marylee Wiley and David Wiley. National Council on Foreign Language and International Studies, 605 Third Avenue, 17th Floor, New York, New York, 10158

Strengthening International Studies in Schools: A Directory of Organizations. Social Studies Development Center, Indiana University, Bloomington, Indiana 47405

Part IV:

MANAGING RENEWAL: OF YOURSELF, YOUR ORGANIZATION, AND OTHERS

The Need
for Renewal

Renewal is a critical life function. Our bodies are physically renewing themselves constantly as we sleep or recover from mental and physical crises. We also need psychological renewal. Like our physical renewal, this is necessary on an ongoing basis, in the form of nurturing, and periodically in deeper reflection on the direction, meaning, and style of our lives and our activities.

Organizations also need renewal—on an ongoing and a periodic basis. Ongoing organizational renewal involves monitoring the health of financial resources, fine-tuning and adjusting for overexpenditure in one area versus another, the reallocation of funds to bolster a project that appears unable to succeed on its own.

Organizational renewal also involves being attentive to human resources. People need words of support and encouragement, guidance and direction, recognition for work well done. Rosabeth Moss Kanter, in her best-selling analysis of the need for renewal in ten major U.S. corporations, *The Change Masters: Innovation for Productivity in the American Corporation,* reports that attention to human resources is becoming the key to the renewal of corporate America. She notes:

> In every sector, old and new, I hear renewed recognition of the importance of people, and of the talents and contributions of individuals, to a company's success. People seem to matter in direct proportion to an awareness of corporate crisis. . . . Indeed, only when an organization exists in stable circumstances, when operations resemble clockwork,

191

unvarying in their practices, can individuals be taken for granted or ignored. . . .

But as world events disturb the smooth workings of corporate machines and threaten to overwhelm us—from OPEC and foreign competition to inflation and deregulation—the number of "exceptions" and change requirements go up, and companies must rely more and more on their people to make decisions on matters for which a routine response may not exist. Thus, individuals actually need to count for more, because it is people within the organization who come up with new ideas, who develop creative responses, and who push for change before opportunities disappear or minor irritants turn into catastrophes. Innovations, whether in products, market strategies, technological processes, or work practices, are designed not by machines but by people.[1]

How is innovation and renewal encouraged? What are the strategies for ensuring that your organization and your volunteers will be responsive to changes that occur within your community and the world? Let us examine the components of personal and organizational renewal.

ORGANIZATIONAL NURTURING: THE NEED FOR ONGOING RENEWAL

Nurturing involves supporting and encouraging the development of a person, organization, or system. It is caring, attentive concern that is tuned into emotional needs. In some ways it is an essential task of leadership to sense the rhythm and pace of your group, the needs of your volunteers and the environment around you, and knowing when and how to make the changes necessary to keep various parts of your group in tune with one another and with the job to be done.

There is an interesting synergy existing among people who are working together effectively toward a common purpose. It is almost a "humming" that you can feel. When some part of your organization gets out of step, it is important for you to be aware of it, sensitive to the reasons for it, and flexible enough to take the action necessary to correct whatever is wrong.

Nurturing actions can take many forms. They can involve encouragement and support. They can also involve guidance and discipline. Nurturing should not be seen as "soft," because it does not relate to content, but process. Nurturing is not whether you are encouraging or disciplining, but what the *result* of your action is on the other person or the organization. Nurturing is a *results-oriented* activity—it must result in a sense of renewal, a new capacity, new skill, new potential to get the job done. If actions debilitate, undermine self-confidence, increase weakness and insecurity, and instill fear, they are not nurturing.

Organizational nurturing is another way of describing organizational leadership. It involves actions that give people a new sense of strength and new visions of their potential. These may consist of challenges, but never challenges that are unreasonable. They may consist of negative feedback, but never negative feedback that is destructive. Nurturing leadership is sensitive to changes and the need for mid-course corrections that allow systems to continue to function in an effective and efficient manner.

We have discussed your nurturing responsibility many times throughout this book. To summarize, a leader's ongoing responsibilities for nurturing an organization are as follows:

SELF–NURTURING

We started our exploration of volunteer management with some of Carl Rogers's observations on effective interpersonal relations. You may remember that Rogers started with himself—assessing what he needed to be open, accepting, aware, and in touch with himself and other people with whom he worked.

In these times of overextension and overcommitment, each of us needs to learn how to be self-nurturing, both for ourselves and for others with whom we work and live, to listen to what our bodies and emotions are saying to us. When we need to rest, we should do it, not push ourselves endlessly to such a point of exhaustion that we reduce our ability to be sensitive to the needs of others and reduce our effectiveness in working with them.

We have also seen throughout this book that international exchange programs offer a wide range of opportunities to develop ourselves in other ways. There are chances for you to expand your awareness of the world, increase your understanding of the "transformations" underway in American society, and extend your understanding of the importance of mission to your organization and your own sense of purpose in the world.

So . . . the first responsibility of us in attempting to lead an organization through renewal is to renew ourselves through care for ourselves in order that we can care for others.

NURTURING OTHERS

In our discussions of leadership, volunteer motivation, cross-cultural communications and counseling, and the management of program operations, I have stressed the importance of being sensitive to the needs which other people encounter through volunteering. What are their needs for affiliation, recognition, or achievement? What life stage are they facing—establishing their own identity, dealing with separation and anxiety in personal relations, building new insights into their life and world events? Nurturing others begins with understanding them and their needs as you work with them to maximize their contribution to your organization's work.

Once you are sensitive to others' needs, you can find appropriate ways to respond. We talked about responding to others' needs in our chapters on leadership and counseling. Appropriate response requires both support and direction. It involves the capacity to be directive when necessary as well as the ability to delegate when people are able to manage tasks for themselves. As we have discussed, this requires flexibility in your leadership style and a capacity to change that style based upon your analysis of the needs of the situation and the people with whom you are working. In such cases, nurturing involves being careful not to put people in situations in which they are over their heads—either in terms of their time or in terms of their skills and abilities.

NURTURING YOUR ORGANIZATION

Everything I have said thus far about nurturing yourself is equally true of the organization you represent. To truly lead a group you have to think of it as a living human being. Groups and organizations, like people, need times for hard work, times for play, times for direction, times for independent creativity, times for support and development, times to fight, and times to make up.

As you examine your organization and its day-to-day functioning, does it have balance in the way it operates? The key to organizational balance is "planning." Thinking ahead and anticipating problems and difficulties, ensuring advance coordination and the effective utilization of human and financial resources is the essence of organizational nurturing. Effective planning is directed toward ensuring that organizational resources are efficiently applied and not wasted by having to play "catch-up" in an unsatisfying, haphazard, and inefficient manner.

If planning can keep an organization on course efficiently and effectively, it is then a primary nurturing mechanism for ongoing organizational renewal.

The nurturing function thus allows you, your people, and your organization to balance your various systems—personal, interpersonal, and organizational. This is a constantly renewing, self-correcting process. And you, as a leader of your group, are the key to ensuring that renewal is a part of the life of your people and your organization—the buck stops with you on this one.

ORGANIZATIONAL REFLECTION: THE NEED FOR PERIODIC EVALUATION OF REVOLUTIONS AND TRANSFORMATIONS

Change within our lives—be it our own lives or the lives of our organizations—can come in two ways. It can be forced upon us from without by changes in our environment, or it can come from within as a result of a conscious, deliberate process of self-evaluation and review. I firmly believe that it is the responsibility of every individual and organization to recurrently engage in a period of reflection in order to ensure that change is planned ahead rather than decided quickly as a reaction to unforeseen circumstances.

One reason I hold this philosophy so strongly is because of the pervasiveness of the changes I described in Chapter 7 as ten current "transformations" of American society and the world. In an earlier draft of this chapter I had called these changes revolutions. But when I reviewed them I realized that many had been underway for almost twenty years and that they all seem still to be "settling out" in terms of their true implications for the future.

Such sea changes in the life of a society may be revolutionary in their results, but they are not revolutionary in process, because they lack the speed and resistance normally associated with a revolution. Instead, these transformations are making their way into the life of the society through slow infusions on many fronts. The government, in fact, has been the chief instigator of some of them.

These changes, developing over a long period, are often not observable on a day-to-day basis. This is one of the reasons for the popularity of Naisbitt's book on megatrends, for he has identified and articulated for people "feelings" they had about things that they had not been able to see clearly before.

One of the advantages of revolutions from the perspective of planning and renewal is that they slap you in the face—you can't miss them. One of the disadvantages is that they may be moving so fast and hard that you may not have a chance to reposition yourself to deal with them effectively.

Transformations, on the other hand, do not slap you in the face. They can sneak up on you in such a way that by the time you notice them it's too late for you and your organization to respond effectively. So each kind of change presents problems.

There are two ways in which to protect yourself and your organization against revolutions and transformations.

For protection against revolutions, you increase security and develop contingency plans. Your "security" for your local exchange group consists of being aware of what is going on in your community and in the international exchange field in order to see any major changes as they are coming. Your contingency planning involves an examination of your areas of greatest vulnerability so as to develop the means to protect yourself against potential disruption through loss. Given the nature of volunteer efforts, this vulnerability is probably to a person or persons—a key volunteer or a key donor.

Protection against transformations can best be found in periodic, systematic evaluation and review of your organization's mission, programs, and activities, as we discussed in the last chapter. The greatest protection against transformation problems, however, lies in the periodic reexamination of your mission. For it is through mission that organizations relate their activities to the sea changes of a nation and the world.

WHEN AND WHAT TO CHANGE

It is easy to say that the best time for change is when it is necessary. However, many of us are so busy implementing programs and running organizations that we sometimes don't realize when change *is* necessary. As protection against stagnation, we need to establish methods for ensuring two kinds of change—ongoing and periodic, based on the nurturing and reflection functions we have already discussed.

To repeat, ongoing responses to change come from day-to-day monitoring of the programs, people, and finances of your organization to ensure that the needs of your visitors, your volunteers, and the purpose of your organization continue to be fulfilled. Peters and Waterman, in their best-selling book, *In Search of Excellence,* called this day-to-day personal monitoring MBWA—Management By Wandering Around. It's being seen, giving small encouragements, asking questions, caring—keeping your fingers on the pulse of your organization, your people, and your activities.

Changes arising from ongoing monitoring will often involve changes that could not have been planned in advance. These may call for a shift in personnel, a change of program activities, a change in structure or an adjustment in your budget. Ongoing changes should never alter the mission or purpose of your organization, for this requires deeper reflection and evaluation.

Periodic responses to change result from a more systematic review, usually at the year's end, when program evaluations have been completed, the financial results are known, and you can sit down with your volunteers and examine your successes and problems. At least four areas of your chapter's work should be considered.

ORGANIZATION MISSION

Has there been a change in your community during the year that has created new needs your organization should try to meet? Have there been changes that have eliminated the need for some services you have been providing?

PROGRAM ACTIVITIES

How successful were your programs? Did they achieve their intended objectives? Should there be new program activities that might meet other needs in your community? Should there be a special emphasis this year?

ORGANIZATION STRUCTURE

Is the structure of your current organization adequate to meet the program needs you see ahead? Are there changes that should be made to allow for any special emphasis this year?

PEOPLE

Is it time for change in the people who handle various jobs? Have some of them been in their positions too long, so that they lack new perspectives, insights and creativity with regard to their responsibilities? Are others too busy with new outside commitments to continue their work? Should *you* step down and give someone else a chance?

All of these questions can be answered during the process of assessing needs that we discussed in Chapter 3 as the first step of the planning process. If you refer back to that chapter, you will see that "organizational renewal" could well have been its title, except for the fact that we did not have a cycle behind us against which to examine renewal.

RISK–TAKING: THE KEY TO RENEWAL

The willingness to take a risk is the key to most change—personal as well as organizational. Once a need has been identified, if it is a significant need for change, the response will inevitably involve some kind of risk—for you, for your organization, or for both. The lack of willingness or ability to take risks is the single most important factor in personal and organizational ineffectiveness and decline. Where does resistance to risk-taking come from and what can we do about it?

I said earlier that most resistance to change arises from fear. The biggest fears that prevent us from taking risks are the flip sides of our motivational drives. Those of us with the need for achievement are prevented from taking risks by a fear of failure. Those of us driven by the need for affiliation are prevented from taking risks by the fear of being rejected. And those of us motivated by a desire for recognition are prevented from taking risks by our fear of loss of status and prestige.

Like individuals, organizations also have their own fears which are very similar. Organizations are prevented from taking risks because of their fear of hurting their reputation. They are afraid of losing the support of donors and volunteers. And they can be afraid of losing the security and efficiency of running their programs in the way that has proven successful over the years.

We all know intellectually that it is impossible to remove risk from life. At the same time, each of us has a "threshold of risk" beyond which we seem to become more cautious—in some cases even paralyzed. The key to ensuring continued renewal and growth for ourselves and the organizations we represent is to be sure that our "risk thresholds" correspond to the thresholds necessary for our organizations to be able to respond effectively to changes in the environment.

THE BASE RATE OF CHANGE

This "base rate of change" is a term I have coined to describe the phenomenon of change as a constant force in our lives. It is not only constant, but accelerating, with change occurring at a faster rate than ever before during any other peace time—from 3 percent to 5 percent to 10 percent to 15 percent in the last several decades. I use the concept of "base rate of change" to parallel "base rates of inflation and unemployment," which are also used to show the lowest feasibly expected level of social and economic phenomena, even during periods of prosperity.

Toffler has written about "future shock" and Naisbitt about "mega-trends." Both have worked to try to identify short- and long-term trends that have contributed to an accelerating rate of change affecting our personal and organizational lives. The ten transformations we identified earlier are also a reflection of this phenomenon.

This high base rate of change affects all of us by requiring us to change our threshold of risk-taking to keep up as the rate accelerates. We need to do this merely to survive. If we want to be creative leaders in the forefront of our field, we will need an additional investment of "risk" to stay ahead.

The result is that we are all faced with increased pressure to understand our personal capabilities and our organizational capacities better. To accomplish this, we need better management—of ourselves and our organizations. This is one of the reasons this guide has been prepared.

RISK–TAKING AND YOUR PERSONAL PHILOSOPHY

As you consider the relationship between yourself and your organization and your ability to respond to change through nurturing and reflection, it might be useful to end where we started, with some final thoughts to add to the seven learnings from Carl Rogers that we examined during Chapter 1. As in Chapter 1, I have added my own observations after each quotation from Rogers.

> Learning 8: "It has been my experience that persons have a basically positive direction."

My instinct is to trust a person whom I am meeting for the first time. Sometimes I am naïve, but I have found that it is a more rewarding experience to begin trusting somebody immediately, and to continue trusting that individual until I have a reason not to, than to start from the opposite direction and wait until the person has proved worthy of my trust.

As a result of this philosophy, I get burned from time to time. But in the long run, I have concluded that I would rather build my life around the 95 percent of the people that I can trust than the 5 that I can't. It makes me and my approach to others more effective, for I do not have to spend my time and energy thinking about ways to protect myself, but can take that creativity and apply it to ways in which I can use my relationship with others to contribute to my own development, to them, and to our common life together.

I guess I have faith in people. Since people are the essence of international exchanges, and I am committed to helping them work together across personal, cultural, and national differences, I can't imagine positioning my life in a way that does not assume that people move in a "basically positive direction." If I couldn't say that and live it, I don't know how I could do what I am doing.

I have also found it helpful in leadership to assume that people move in a positive direction in their lives. This has allowed me to give them much more responsibility and to take more risks than I might have otherwise. It has also allowed opportunities for personal growth and development to the people involved that they might not otherwise have had.

If I were to assume that people move in a negative direction, I would have to structure an organization with controls to protect people from themselves and to protect the organization from their potential malevolence. Aside from making the organization a bad place to work, it seems that this would be prohibitively expensive and just a poor use of resources.

I do not want to be misinterpreted as being Pollyanna-ish, for I am very aware that people, in defensiveness and fear, strike out at others and often strike out at me in ways that can be very cruel, regressive, antisocial, and hurtful. Yet I repeat that I would prefer to find this out by exception than to assume that all people approach me with hostility at the outset.

> Learning 9: "Life, at best, is a flowing, changing process in which nothing is fixed."

In my work with others, I have found that life is most rewarding when it is dynamic and changing. This means that I have to learn to live with uncertainty and have to accept the fact that what was important for me yesterday may not be as important today, and what will be important for me tomorrow may also need to be different.

It means that I cannot hold onto the past, cannot protect the procedures and operations of my organization, which were relevant to another time and place, from the new demands of today. It means that I must be constantly aware of what new needs are being created and what new opportunities the world is offering.

It is not easy to live in such a state of fluidity. But once I accepted change as a constant state and learned to expect flux rather than order, I found a peace of mind that allows me to enjoy the challenge of dramatic events occurring around me. I trust it may have allowed me also to be a little less defensive and resistant to changes that are suggested to me, either for my organization or for myself.

WHERE DO WE GO FROM HERE?

Your involvement in international exchanges is a positive statement of your commitment to the world and a vision of the possibilities of peaceful coexistence and international understanding. It is a
statement of your concern about people, your belief in their potential,
and your recognition that we must all look beyond ourselves if we are
to gain the best from life for ourselves and those we love.

In this guide I have tried to encourage you, challenge you, stretch
you, and help you think about the work in which we are all engaged. I
have suggested that you need to believe in yourself and in others, and
be sensitive to your own needs and the needs of others in developing
an organization that meets the needs of your community and the
needs of the international visitors whom you serve.

As we bring this journey to an end, I want to share with you what
has kept me involved in international exchange, even after I have left
it as a full-time professional endeavor. My guess is that you, too, have
your own memory that has kept you involved over the years.

My memory is of the AFS students gathering together in one place
after the end of a year in the United States. We had almost three
thousand of them, from sixty countries, in a large high school gymna-
sium for a final "goodbye speech" which I delivered before they left to
go to the chartered aircraft waiting at a nearby airport to fly them to
their respective homes. Nothing remains with me more from my years
with AFS and my travels around the world than these teenagers from
sixty countries embracing, crying, laughing, and saying goodbye to
one another. If the promises made on that day could be kept for the
next fifty years, the world would be a very different place and we
would be better able to meet the challenges that lie ahead.

But, even if the promises are not kept and the memories fade, no
one will ever be able to take away from these young people (or from
me) the fact that we have experienced a world community. We have
seen that people from different nations *can* come together and live
together, work together, and laugh together. Perhaps, if nothing more,
that experience will give us all hope as we face the staggering challenges awaiting us.

Perhaps it will help us to believe that someday the people of the
world will be able to better work together, because people like us
have helped them experience other ways of life. Through interna-

tional exchange programs such as yours and mine we have seen that international cooperation *is* possible, we have learned to care about people in other nations, and we have taken one small step toward becoming members of a true world community. . . .

Thank you for all you are doing to enable others to Bring Home the World.

For Further Study

Burns, James MacGregor. *Leadership.* New York: Harper & Row, 1978.

Drucker, Peter F. *Management: Tasks, Responsibilities, Practices.* New York: Harper & Row, 1974.

_____. *Managing in Turbulent Times.* New York: Harper & Row, 1980.

Kanter, Rosabeth Moss. *The Change Masters: Innovation for Productivity in the American Corporation.* New York: Simon & Schuster, 1983.

Kimberly, John R., Robert H. Miles and Associates. *The Organizational Life Cycle: Issues in the Creation, Transformation and Decline of Organizations.* San Francisco: Jossey-Buss Publishers, 1981.

Peters, Thomas J. and Robert H. Waterman, Jr. *In Search of Excellence.* New York: Harper & Row, 1982.

Rogers, Carl. *On Becoming a Person.* New York: Houghton-Mifflin, 1961.

APPENDICES

Appendix I

Organizations Sponsoring International Exchange and Global Education Programs

I. International Exchange Organizations

AFS International/Intercultural Programs
313 East 43rd Street
New York, New York 10017

AIESEC (*Association Internationale des Etudiants en Sciences Economiques et Commerciales*, the International Association of Students in Economics and Business Management)
14 West 23rd Street
New York, New York 10010

American Institute for Foreign Study Scholarship Foundation
102 Greenwich Avenue
Greenwich, Connecticut 06830

American Intercultural Student Exchange
7728 Lookout Drive
LaJolla, California 92037

American Scandinavian Student Exchange
228 North Coast Highway
Laguna Beach, California 92651

American Secondary Schools for International Students and Teachers
Stonecrest Farm
Wilder, Vermont 05088

American Youth Hostels, Inc.
1332 I Street, Suite 800
Washington, D.C. 20005

Amigos De Las Americas
5618 Star Lane
Houston, Texas 77057

The Carl Duisberg Society
425 Park Avenue
New York, New York 10022

Children's International Summer Villages, Inc.
USA National Office
206 North Main Street
Casstown, Ohio 45312

Council on International Educational Exchange
205 East 42nd Street
New York, New York 10017

Council of International Programs
1030 Euclid Avenue, Suite 410
Cleveland, Ohio 44115

Earthwatch
10 Juniper Road
Belmont, Mass. 02178

Educational Foundation for Foreign Study
1528 Chapala Street
Santa Barbara, CA 93101

The Experiment in International Living
Kipling Road
Brattleboro, Vermont 05301

Future Farmers of America
P.O. Box 15160
Alexandria, Virginia 22309

German American Partnership Program
Goethe House New York
1014 Fifth Avenue
New York, New York 10028

IAESTE Trainee Program
Association for International Practical Training
217 American City Building
Columbia, Maryland 21044

International Christian Youth Exchange
134 West 26th Street
New York, New York 10001

International Student Exchange Program
   Georgetown University
1236 36th Street, NW
Washington, D.C. 20547

Institute of International Education
809 United Nations Plaza
New York, New York 10017

Mobility International, USA
P.O. Box 3551
Eugene, Oregon 97403

NACEL Cultural Exchange
510 10th Avenue, N.E.
Stewartville, Minnesota 55976

National Association for Foreign Student Affairs
1860 19th Street, NW
Washington, D.C. 20009

National Council for International Visitors
Meridian House
1630 Crescent Place, N.W.
Washington, D.C. 20009

National 4-H Council
7100 Connecticut Avenue
Chevy Chase, Maryland 20815

Open Door Student Exchange
124 East Merrick Road
Valley Stream, New York 11582

Operation Crossroads Africa, Inc.
150 Fifth Avenue, Suite 310
New York, New York 10011

Pacific American International Student Services
244 California Street, Suite 206
San Francisco, California 94111

Partners of the Americas
1424 K Street, NW
Suite 700
Washington, D.C. 20005

People-to-People International
2420 Pershing Road
Suite 300
Kansas City, Missouri 64108

Rotary International
1600 Ridge Avenue
Evanston, IL 60201

School Exchange Service
National Association of Secondary School Principals
1904 Association Drive
Reston, Virginia 22091

Sister Cities International
1625 I Street, NW
Washington, D.C. 20006

Spanish Heritage
116-53 Queens Boulevard
Forest Hills, New York 11375

YMCA International Program Services
236 East 47th Street
New York, New York 10017

Youth Exchange Service
350 South Figueroa
Suite 257P
Los Angeles, California 90071

Youth For Understanding
3501 Newark Street, N.W.
Washington, D.C. 20016

II. Global Education Organizations

Bay Area Global Education Program
Global Perspectives in Education (West Coast Office)
Mills College Station
P.O. Box 9976
Oakland, CA 94613

Center for Public Education in International Affairs
School of International Relations
University of Southern California
Los Angeles, California 90089

Center for Teaching International Relations
University of Denver
University Park
Denver, Colorado 80208

Foreign Policy Association
205 Lexington Avenue
New York, New York 10016

Global Awareness Program
School of Education
Florida International University
Tamiami Trail
Miami, Florida 33199

Global Education Center
110 Pattee Hall
150 Pillsbury Drive, SE
University of Minnesota
Minneapolis, Minnesota 55455

Global Learning Inc.
40 South Fullerton Avenue
Montclair, New Jersey 07042

Global Perspectives in Education, Inc.
218 East 18th Street
New York, New York 10003

Las Palomas de Taos
P.O. Box 3194
Taos, New Mexico 87571

Mershon Center
Citizenship Development and Global Education Program
199 West 10th Avenue
Columbus, Ohio 43201

Social Studies Development Center
2805 East Tenth Street
Indiana University
Bloomington, Indiana 47405

Appendix II

Examples of Model Global Education Activities

A few examples of activities that have worked in various communities around the United States may be useful as you consider entering this aspect of international exchange work. Here are some recent experiences, many of which have been recognized by the National Association for Foreign Student Affairs (NAFSA) as outstanding activities utilizing foreign exchange students as global educational resources in local school districts.

Colorado: Foreign Language Festival, Delta County School District, Paonia, Colorado

A two-day Foreign Language Festival was held with foreign exchange students spending one day in each of two district high schools. During the festival foreign students gave presentations about their home countries to language, social studies, home economics, history, English, and physical education classes. Other aspects included: fashion shows of the dress of other countries, narrated in the language of the country; presentations of national songs and dances; international refreshments; and display booths of objects from other countries. The project led to the formation of a foreign language club. An audiovisual tape of the festival was produced.

Georgia: International Celebration, Atlanta Public Schools, Atlanta, Georgia.

A multi-faceted program was conducted consisting of: three cultural evenings organized and attended by students, teachers, parents and community members, which included folk dancing, a cabaret night and a "musical tour" of Germany; six "lunch n' learn" programs, held in the library and hosted by consular wives and foreign students, which provided an opportunity for cross-cultural sharing and information; three days of instruction on the "two Germanys," in which the German Consulate cooperated with history and social studies teachers; and an international luncheon, attended by representatives of ten youth exchange organizations, several civic groups, students of the Exchange Council who had received scholarships for summer study abroad and teachers. An audiovisual tape of the week was produced for future use.

Michigan: Social and Cultural Programs for U.S. and Foreign Exchange Students, Volunteers for International Hospitality Programs, Ann Arbor, Michigan.

Foreign and U.S. high school students were invited to participate in several organized visits: a baseball game, preceded by a picnic and followed by a discussion with the players and the coach; an evening of aerobic exercises and folk dancing from many cultures; a tour through an art museum followed by a reception; and a visit to Greenfield Village, a large outdoor museum featuring period shops, work places, carriages, trains, and the homes of famous Americans like Thomas Edison and Henry Ford. As part of the regular faculty meeting, the program also offered a short teacher training session stressing the value of foreign students as important resources in the teaching/learning process. An audiovisual tape of these activities was also made.

New York: International Club Activities, Brighton Central Schools, Rochester, New York.

Field trips to area centers of industry and business, agriculture, recreation, arts and history were conducted for foreign and U.S. students of Brighton High School's International Club. The club also organized an International Week at the school, which included activities such as placing signs in the foreign language of the day over the existing signs at the library, administrative offices, restrooms, etc. and starting the morning public address announcements with greetings in the foreign language of the day. International foods were a part of each day's cafeteria menu and special presentations were made by the foreign students of dance, art, native dress, and slides. The week consisted of an Eastern Europe Day and India Day, Europe Day, Middle East Day, the Americas Day, and a Far East Day. An audiovisual tape was produced.

Ohio: Resources International, Columbus World Affairs Council, Columbus, Ohio.

Resources International, see Figure 11, is an organization of volunteers from mid-Ohio that includes businessmen and women, researchers, world travelers, university professors, and community volunteers. Started in 1977, it offers speakers and consulting assistance to teachers in Columbus who want to add a personalized international dimension to their classroom activities. Volunteers are prepared to come to the schools to speak on a wide range of topics, world issues, and geographic areas. It is exactly the kind of endeavor, trying to bring teachers and resources together through a volunteer broker, that I have been encouraging you to consider throughout this chapter.

Wisconsin: Exchange Students as Resources: in the Classroom and the Community, School District of Superior, Superior, Wisconsin.

Three students—one from Finland, West Germany, and Switzerland—were enrolled in the Superior, Wisconsin, school district in 1983–84. Brochures were distributed throughout the community to publicize the availability of these foreign students for public presentations. A highlight of their visit was a community reception held in collaboration with the Rotary Club of Superior. Community leaders such as the mayor, the executive secretary of the Chamber of Commerce, and the editor of the local newspaper attended. The exchange students were introduced and each made a short presentation about her home country and the appreciation she has gained for the United States during her visit. Videotapes were made of each of the students' presentations, which along with other information about their country was contributed to form the beginning of an international resource file in the school library, which will be available in future years to students and community organizations interested in learning more about these countries.

These programs are just a few examples of hundreds of innovative activities across the United States that are being developed daily to increase the use of foreign visitors.

NOTES

Notes

Chapter 1

1. Brian O'Connell. *Effective Leadership in Voluntary Organizations* (New York: McGraw-Hill, 1981), p. xii.

2. Carl Rogers. *On Becoming a Person* (New York: Houghton-Mifflin, 1961), pp. 15–17.

3. I believe the use of the male reference (he, his, and him) as a general pronoun over the years has contributed to sexist views. In this volume, therefore, I am randomly using the female pronoun (she, hers, and her) in order to offset this bias.

4. Dr. Darold A. Treffert. "Mellowing: An Alternative to Coping" (Fond du Lac, Wisc: Brookside Medical Center, 1980), p. 4.

Chapter 2

1. Charles F. MacCormack. "International Youth Exchange: Completing the Public Policy Agenda," ITT/American University Lecture on the Future of Public Diplomacy, (Brattleboro, Vt.: The Experiment in International Living, 1984), p. 4.

2. William Fulbright. "Speech Before the 1983 Annual Conference of the Council on International Educational Exchange" (New York: CIEE, 1983), p. 3.

Chapter 3

1. Peter F. Drucker. *The Effective Executive* (New York: Harper & Row, 1966). p. 23ff.

2. David C. McClelland. "Achievement Motivation Can Be Developed," *Harvard Business Review* (November–December, 1965).

Chapter 4

1. Chester I. Barnard. *The Functions of the Executive* (Cambridge, Mass.: Harvard University Press, 1938).

2. Karl Mathiasen III. "The Board of Directors of Nonprofit Organizations" (Washington, D.C.: Center for Community Change, 1977), p. 16.

3. _____. "No Board of Directors Is Like Any Other: Some Maxims About Boards" (Washington, D.C.: Center for Community Change, 1982), p. 9.

4. The best-known book on corporate culture is *In Search of Excellence* (New York: Harper & Row, 1982) by Thomas R. Peters and Robert L. Waterman, Jr. Other excellent, but lesser-known books on the subject include *Corporate Cultures: The Rites and Rituals of Corporate Life* (Reading, Mass.: Addison-Wesley, 1982) by Terrence E. Deal and Allan A. Kennedy; *Managing Corporate Culture* (Cambridge, Mass.: Ballinger Publishing Company, 1984) by Stanley M. Davis, and *Creating Excellence: Managing Corporate Culture, Strategy and Change in the New Age* (New York: New American Library, 1984) by Craig R. Hickman and Michael A. Silva.

5. Figure 3, "Characteristics of Healthy and Unhealthy Volunteer Chapters" has been adapted from a similar guide by Jack K. Fordyce and Raymond Weil in *Managing People* (Reading, Mass.: Addison-Wesley, 1971), pp. 11–14.

Chapter 5

1. "1983 Gallup Survey on Volunteering," *Voluntary Action Leadership* (Winter 1984), pp. 20–22.

2. McClelland's groundbreaking work in this area is *The Achieving Society* (Princeton, N.J.: Van Nostrand, 1961).

3. For the general theory of situational leadership, see Paul Hersey and Kenneth Blanchard. *Management of Organizational Behavior: Utilizing Human Resources.* 3rd ed. (Englewood Cliffs, N.J.: Prentice-Hall, 1977).

4. This small book is written for a popular audience and has been widely used and adapted for communications between parents and teenagers and other groups. The basic allegory is contained in Kenneth Blanchard and Spencer Johnson, *The One Minute Manager* (New York: William Morrow and Company, 1982).

5. This list has been adapted from an outline by Marlene Wilson in her book, *The Effective Management of Volunteer Programs* (Boulder, Colorado: Volunteer Management Associates, 1976), pp. 115–119.

Chapter 8

1. In most not-for-profit community organizations, basic accounting and tax functions are handled by someone with a background in these fields. For this reason, I shall not deal in depth in these areas. I am also not going to cover whether or how to incorporate and apply for tax-exempt status. Many small volunteer committees in the international exchange field are covered under an umbrella tax exemption by their national organization. If you are interested in learning more about local incorporation and tax exemption, consult Chapters 5–8 of Joan Flanagan's excellent book, *The Successful Volunteer Organization* (Chicago: Contemporary Books, 1981).

2. Flanagan, *op. cit.,* pp. 284–85.

Chapter 9

1. Brian O'Connell. *Effective Leadership in Voluntary Organizations.* (New York: Walker and Company, 1981), p. 179.

Chapter 10

1. See Robert Hanvey. *Attaining a Global Perspective* (New York: Global Perspectives in Education, 1975), p. 7.

2. Edward T. Hall. *Beyond Culture* (Garden City, N.Y.: Doubleday & Company, Inc., 1976), p. 79.

Chapter 11

1. Gerard Egan. *The Skilled Helper* (Monterey, California: Brooks/ Cole Publishing Company, 1982).

2. From "Cross-cultural Counseling" by David Horner and Kay Vandersluis in *Learning Across Cultures* (Washington, D.C.: National Association of Foreign Student Affairs, 1981), pp. 37–38.

3. (Indianapolis, Ind.: Bobbs-Merrill, 1975), pp. 19–31.

4. Ray Birdwhistell. *Kinesics and Content* (Philadelphia: University of Pennsylvania Press, 1970).

Chapter 12

1. Frank Rosengren, Marylee Crofts Wiley and David S. Wiley. *Internationalizing Your School: A Handbook & Resource Guide for Teachers, Administrators, Parents and School Board Members* (New York: National Council on Foreign Languages and International Studies, 1983), p. 2.

2. Linda Reed. "Internationally Experienced Students . . . A Valuable Resource" mimeographed (Washington, D.C.: National Association for Foreign Student Affairs, 1984), p. 2.

3. *Ibid.,* pp. 6–8.

4. This was one of the findings of research by Mary Anne Flournoy, "Omar, You Have Changed My World: Making the Most of Interna-

tional Visitors in the Classroom" mimeographed (Athens, Ohio: Ohio Valley International Council, 1984).

5. *The AFS Impact Study* in four reports by Neal Grove and Bettina Hansel is available from the AFS Research Department, AFS International/Intercultural Programs, 313 East 43rd Street, New York, New York 10017. The YFU research is available from YFU Research Department, Youth For Understanding, 3501 Newark St., N.W., Washington, D.C. 20016.

6. Angene H. Wilson. "Exchange Students as Bridges Between Cultures" (Louisville, Ky.: University of Kentucky, 1984), p. 5.

7. Description taken from Josef A. Mestenhauser. "Foreign Students as Teachers: Lessons from the Program in Learning with Foreign Students," *Learning Across Cultures* (Washington, D.C.: National Association for Foreign Student Affairs, 1981), p. 146.

8. *A Place Called School* (New York: McGraw-Hill Book Company, 1983), pp. 212–213.

Chapter 13

1. Rosabeth Moss Kanter. *The Change Masters* (New York: Simon & Schuster, 1983), p. 17.